What is capit
Can it last?

A book of readings

Edited by Cathy Nugent

Phoenix Press 2012
ISBN 978-0-9531864-5-7

Phoenix Press
Workers' Liberty
20E Tower Workshops
Riley Road
London, SE1 3DG

Contents

Fighting the Tories: what next?

By Daniel Randall and Martin Thomas

After the sudden crash of 2008-9 bankers' and bosses' pay and bonuses, share prices, and profits recovered nicely. But there was been no economic recovery for the working class. Real wages are going down, and set to go down further. Unemployment is high and still rising. The Government plans even heavier cuts for the next few years than it has made in 2010-2.

And the economic picture globally (with a slowdown in China and high oil prices) and in Europe determines that the prospect is gloomy. At best we are heading for a long period of economic depression, or possibly for fresh shocks which will crash even the superficial semi-recovery (for the bourgeoisie only) and a limited revival of private-sector jobs.

Capitalist slumps coming after a period of relatively low working-class activity and confidence usually, in the first place, push down activity and confidence further. The militant working-class expression of the anger, disillusionment, and enforced rethinking generated by the slump usually comes not in the midst of the slump, but in the subsequent economic recovery or general semi-recovery.

That is the general (though not invariable) rule, and it is no surprise that things have, broadly, worked that way so far in this crisis.

Even so, it matters a great deal whether the setbacks in living standards, working conditions, organisation, confidence, and class cohesion suffered in the slump are limited or large. It matters whether partial victories, and limited initiatives to rebuild, can be established in the slump, or not. It matters whether the socialists can recruit the individuals pushed by slump times into re-thinking, and educate them, train them, integrate them.

The 30 June and 30 November 2011 strikes made the organised working class a visible social force in a way not seen in a generation. The great many young workers who struck for the first time on 30 June or 30 November will have learned about the power of organised labour.

The problem with the pensions dispute has not been that workers were unwilling to move.

The 30 June and 30 November strikes, and even the 28 March 2012 teach-

3

ers' strike (confined to London, and called as a "sop" by union leaders who had already overruled union membership surveys calling for a national strike), got good responses. The demonstrations on those strike days brought out large numbers of workers, especially young workers.

There is every reason to suppose that if the union leaders had allowed more honest and open communications, and real debate, then large suppressed resources of creativity, imagination, criticism, and militancy among the rank and file would have been released.

But the pensions dispute is now ailing, on life support with the 10 May day of action and vague talk of something more in late June. This is a significant setback. The union leaders have been found wanting; and, in certain ways, the movement as a whole has been found wanting too.

The pensions dispute, paradoxically, has encouraged decline for the local anti-cuts committees which mushroomed from late 2010. Committees were swivelled towards focusing on "the next big thing" (26 March, 30 June, 30 November), and then left limp after the "big thing"; or undercut by the focusing of activist energies on the pensions issue, on which, given the unions' complete lack in practice of a political campaign to accompany their industrial action, the anti-cuts committees had little traction. In most though not all areas those local anti-cuts committees are significantly reduced.

We must learn lessons from the shortcomings of the pensions campaign:

• Almost total lack of debate in the unions about strategy; indeed almost total lack of honest communication from union leaders to their members during the campaign.

• Bad effects of a trade union approach which, amidst a vast welter of attacks by government and bosses on workers' conditions, handed down from above a focus on one hoped-for "making-a-breach" issue (pensions) and a series of one-off protests on that issue.

• Lack of a public political campaign, linking the issues of public-sector pensions with those of private-sector pensions and the state pension.

• Bad effects of a trade union culture which has come to see strikes as one-off protests to strengthen union officials' hands in subsequent negotiations, rather than as continuous action to force concessions. There has been a habit of seeing strikes, when they happened, as "about" pensions, rather than for specific demands.

This culture also sees ballots on strikes more as gambits in negotiations than as instructions by the members to union leaders.

• The paralysing effect of a doctrine, proclaimed most vocally by the PCS leaders, that unions cannot hope to achieve anything even on the details of their own members' pay, jobs, and conditions, unless they get other unions to strike alongside them.

• Weakness of the major "left" or "rank and file" groups in all the unions involved — STA and CDFU in the NUT, Left Unity in PCS, Unison United

Left, Unite United Left — which failed to suggest strategies different from the top leaders' and to promote debate.

• Even hard-core activist left groups such as the Socialist Workers Party and Socialist Party expressed a distinct view chiefly through proposing that the actions promised or planned by the leaders (30 June, 30 November, etc.) be thought of in more radical terms (as a "one-day public sector general strike"), or thought of as leading straight into more radical action ("two-day general strike" or "all out, stay out"), or thought of as likely to bring down the government.

The conference on 16 June called by the Local Associations for Action on Pensions has begun the work of establishing a rank-and-file network of school workers.

Over the next years and decades, socialists should focus their work in the unions on not just mobilising the rank and file against the top leaders. It is also a matter of helping to develop, and working with, a new generation of younger union activists, with the aid of the best of the experienced older activists.

The average age of a workplace rep in the British trade union movement was in the late 40s on the most recent comprehensive figures (2004) and will be older now. In other words, the average union rep is someone who probably came into activity around the time of the 1984-5 miners' strike.

The number of workplace reps across the economy has, according to best guesses, dwindled from 335,000 in 1984 to maybe 150,000 in 2004-9 — faster than union membership has declined. On the best guesses available, the proportion of paid union full-time officials to members has increased somewhat, though the total number of paid full-time officials remains small, perhaps 3,000 across the whole movement. On the latest available figures, 81% of paid union full-time officials are over 40.

Today's older union reps who started activity in the 1980s are, in many ways, the best of their generation. They stuck with the movement while others fell away.

Yet many of them — on the evidence of the pensions dispute, a majority of them — have suffered an erosion of spirit, even if they are still nominally left-wing or revolutionary-minded. For twenty or thirty years they have been trained in union activity as damage limitation — as primarily an effort by assiduous union negotiators to get a passable outcome on individual grievances or on redeployments following job cuts. The predominance of older reps often means that younger reps are hegemonised by, and take their model of union activity from, the older ones.

The winning of union facility time, from the 1970s onwards, was a trade union gain, linked with legal guarantees of rights of union representation to workers with grievances. We should defend facility time against the attacks being made by employers and government.

However, we should also recognise that facility time has been a double-edged gain, providing a basis for a sort of "bureaucratisation at rank-and-file level". We must drill down below the layer of long-standing facility-time trade unionists to a wider range of workers.

We should strive constantly to draw newer, younger workers into facility-time activity, and to combat assumptions that once older workers get facility-time posts, they more or less automatically keep them until retirement.

We should work wherever possible to generalise individual grievances into collective ones, rather than letting workplace union activity become an aggregate of atomised individual casework. We should insist on accurate, speedy, and full communication by facility-time reps to the members they represent, and well-organised and democratic meetings to decide policy and monitor their work.

That "trade union activist" usually connotes someone at least middle-aged is not iron law.

The French union movement collects statistics which give us a picture. At the Amiens congress of the CGT in 1906, the average age of delegates was 36. Victor Griffuelhes became general secretary of the whole union confederation at the age of 27; Léon Jouhaux succeeded him at the age of 30; even after World War Two, the crusty Stalinist Georges Séguy became secretary of the CGT railworkers at 22, and secretary of the whole confederation at the age of 40. Around 1961 the average age of CGT congress delegates was 38. The average became markedly younger from 1968 through to 1978, and then rose again. By 2006 it was 48.

A rejuvenation of the corps of union activists is not only possible in the coming years, but necessary. The current generation will move on whatever we do. More and more of the existing activists will move into retirement, early retirement, or ill health.

So far, new young activists roused up by the "new anti-capitalism", by environmental activism, or by the big anti-war mobilisations have not flowed on into union activism in anything like the way the student and youth radicalisation of the late 1960s and early 70s flowed on.

Some activists have moved into the NGO world, and others straight or almost straight from university into being full-time union officials.

Some have remained active in miscellaneous campaigns while relying for income on casual and short-term jobs where they don't do union organising. Yet there must be a larger potential for developing new young union activists than has been realised so far.

The defeat over pensions does not at all wipe out the prospects for working-class struggle in the next year or so. In working-class history it has often happened that what looked in advance like the "main" issue passed with relatively little action; and then an issue which seems secondary or off-centre sparked revolt.

There are plenty of issues coming up: service cuts, pay freezes, radical marketisation of the Health Service, benefit cuts, "new standards" in schools... And there is plenty of discontent to supply the raw material for mobilisation.

The Tories are already following up on the pensions dispute with further attacks:

• the continuing social cuts, as detailed above;

• continued cuts in real wages in the public sector. The current two-year pay freeze will be followed by a one per cent limit on pay rises from 2013-4;

• plans to "regionalise" public sector pay;

• privatisation and marketisation in the health service and in education;

• possible moves in the public sector to cut union facility time, or even in some places to de-recognise unions.

The threat of new anti-union laws also remains on their desk, though currently dormant.

Regional pay will be hard to push through on a large scale. If the average public-sector pay rise is to be limited to one per cent, then it will be hard to open up large differentials between regions without actually cutting nominal wages in the regions destined for lower pay, and historically workers resist cuts in nominal wages much more fiercely than cuts in real wages brought about by price inflation.

Economist Richard Disney, a former IMF adviser who has been called in as an adviser by the Government and who says that regional pay is in general "a good idea", declares: "If you were to do it, you should do it when people are getting three or four per cent increases and someone should have had the courage to recommend it a few years ago. I don't really know how you do it now".

Even modest union mobilisations (and political mobilisations by a Labour Party demagogically using the regional-pay plan to try to regain support in areas like Wales) have a good chance of defeating any large extensions of regional pay. In PCS, the Government's regional-pay plans could be used as a spur to relaunch a rank and file based campaign for national pay, uniting pay rates not only between regions but between the civil service's different negotiating units (currently about 200 in number).

We should look out for two dangers.

First, union leaders may claim a regional pay system with only tiny differentials between regions as pretty much a victory, when in fact the Government has no serious plans for more than tiny differentials in the short run, and is happy to establish the principle and then have the differentials widen gradually over time.

Second, in some sectors localised pay may be a bigger danger than regional pay.

In health, different foundation trusts could pay different rates. In further education, many colleges already vary the national wage rates. In schools, basic national pay rates could be held down, and teachers could be pushed into having to look to bonuses paid by academies (in exchange for worse conditions and longer hours) as the way to improve pay.

As of 1 April 2012 there are 1,776 academies open in England. The total of state schools is about 3,000 secondary and 17,000 primary. Since most academies are secondary schools, this means that around half of all secondary schools are now academies. There were 203 academies in September 2010.

School workers' unions should turn towards organising within academies; developing structures which allow rank-and-file control over union activity across academy chains (like combine committees); and pattern-bargaining-type approaches to defending and improving terms and conditions in academies.

How far from that we are as yet is indicated by the fact that the National Union of Teachers does not even have a reliable count of how many academies it has union recognition in.

The Health and Social Care Act opens the door to full marketisation of health care, and opens a path to the imposition of charges for health care with the government only providing subsidies to limit those charges. (The Spanish government is already moving towards such charges).

However, from opening the door to the process to completing it is a long and cumbersome process, and one in which there will be many opportunities for resistance.

One of the reasons why many Tories seriously proposed dropping the Health and Social Care Bill was that they feared such wildfire resistance, and thought it better to damage the Health Service more stealthily and piecemeal, without a high-profile focus for resistance.

Hospitals will close "unprofitable" sections — or be forced not to close them. Hospitals will divert resources to pulling in more private patients — or be forced not to. Hospitals and other NHS operations will be taken over by the likes of Serco or Virgin — or kept by popular protest within public administration. GPs will hand over commissioning to Serco-type companies, or agree to be accountable to their patients.

Politically, Ed Miliband's talk against "predators" remains unsubstantiated by any more-than-piffling content, and there is as yet no union pressure to make him substantiate it.

Ed Balls and Ed Miliband quickly followed the unions' December 2011 climbdown on pensions by shifting Labour's stance on cuts from an already-weak "opposing these cuts, though we concede there should be slower and smaller cuts" to "accepting the broad sweep of the cuts, but criticising the details and the scale".

Miliband has sought to "rebalance" slightly by declaiming against the Health and Social Care Bill and having health spokesperson Andy Burnham promise to reverse the Tories' damage in the NHS (while Labour has studiously refused to commit to reversing Tory damage in any other social sphere). But the die-hard Blairites have been gathering vigour and influence.

Although the 2011 Labour Party conference had more spirit and dissent on the floor than any other conference for a long time, the organised Labour left remains very weak.

Labour is now much more dependent on trade union money than in the Blair years. We must fight for consistent political self-assertion by the unions — against diplomacy with the Labour leaders as a substitute for confrontation — and against the idea that progress can be better made by breaking the Labour-union link, and thus dodging a fight with the Labour leaders, than by tackling them.

• From *Solidarity* 243, 25 April 2012.

Four programmes for the Euro-crisis

By Martin Thomas

The election results in France and Greece (6 May), and the forced resignation of militantly neo-liberal Dutch prime minister Mark Rutte (23 April), have thrown economic policy in the eurozone into flux

There are four main distinct approaches in play. The debate between them has scarcely started in the British labour movement, where even the would-be Marxist left has so far mostly limited itself to a sort of conservative syndicalism: opposing cuts in Britain, advocating more militant tactics, applauding resistance elsewhere in Europe, and commenting that the EU leaders are making a mess of things.

There is debate in Britain among economists. Jonathan Portes, head of the National Institute of Economic and Social Research, former Chief Economist at the Cabinet Office, and an "establishment" economist if ever there was one, responded to the French and Greek elections by declaring that "the idiots in Brussels", "the austerity crowd", had "lost the arguments", and economic life should now be boosted by a big and concerted programme of public spending on infrastructure (roads, rail, schools, hospitals, housing, other public facilities).

The Marxist left should break from its defensive, hunkered-down stance, and take the debate into the labour movement.

Until now neo-liberal policy has dominated. It proposes that governments which cannot borrow on open global financial markets, or have difficulty doing so, must mend their position by huge social cuts.

It advocates strict budget-balancing even for the better-off countries like Germany and the Netherlands; and, indeed, constitutional amendments across Europe to make balanced budgets compulsory except in extremes. To demands for "growth" it responds that the only way is via "labour market reforms", in other words smashing up workers' rights, making labour markets ultra-flexible for the bosses, cutting social overhead costs.

Like George Osborne's policy in Britain, it is above all a policy for the bosses and bankers to "use" the economic crisis to their advantage, in shifting the balance of class forces further against the working class (and, they hope, permanently) — rather than a policy to ease the crisis.

Its priority, as Angela Merkel put it in December 2011, is to "show [footloose global capital] that Europe is a safe place to invest".

It is an arrogant policy which risks provoking serious nationalist backlashes against the slowly-evolved reduction of barriers within Europe. It means unelected European Union officials monitoring each elected government's budget each year and vetoing it unless it includes enough cuts and marketisations.

There is a Euro-Keynesian approach. It advocates easing the credit difficulties of the Greek and other governments by lending on easy terms from the European Central Bank, or by the issuing of Eurobonds guaranteed by the collective creditworthiness of the eurozone.

It favours a wealth tax to raise revenue, but opposes rapid deficit reduction through social cuts, and says that better-off countries positively should be running large government budget deficits so as to boost market demand across Europe. It calls for audits of government debt, and repudiation of parts of it.

It demands a big expansion of the budget of the European Union itself (as distinct from member states), and EU-financed investment projects in the worse-off countries.

Many left-wing economists advocate the full Euro-Keynesian package. Left social-democrats, notably Syriza in Greece, advocate versions of it. Jean-Luc Mélenchon, the left social-democrat candidate in the French presidential election, said that the European Central Bank must be placed "under democratic control to allow it to lend at low — or even nil — rates, directly to the states, and to buy public debt".

Shreds of Euro-Keynesianism can be found right across the mainstream political spectrum, through François Hollande to the fiercely-cutting "technocrat" Italian prime minister Mario Monti and the IMF, and even in the recent statement by neo-liberal German finance minister Wolfgang Schäuble that "it is fine if wages in Germany currently rise faster than in other EU countries".

At an angle to the range from Schäuble to Syriza are two other approaches: the national-Keynesian and the revolutionary socialist.

Far-right groups like the Front National in France push the most popular version of the national-Keynesian approach: quit the euro, import controls, reindustrialise, more government regulation of the economy and the banks. The FN upholds the interests of smaller-scale French capitalist businesses who orient primarily to France's internal market and are indifferent or hostile to France being a "safe place to invest" for global capital.

A FN government would block migration; scapegoat and harass the immigrant workers already in France; and enforce "government regulation" in the shape of crushing the labour movement and democratic rights.

There is a left-wing version of the national-Keynesian approach, similar to the "Alternative Economic Strategy" popular in Britain's Labour left in

11

the 1970s and 80s. Groups like the KKE in Greece suggest that if countries quit the EU, reimpose controls on trade and capital movements, and use government to promote domestic industry, then the labour movement can win better conditions in the national framework than in a wider one.

Revolutionary socialists agree that no national labour movement should wait for a cross-European movement.

A workers' government in a single country, emerging in advance of a large cross-Europe revolutionary working-class movement, would have no choice but to defy EU rulings and face exclusion from the EU. It would have to use economic border controls to sustain, as best it could, an economy within that country dominated by workers' control and economic equalisation, and to navigate within the world market.

An isolated workers' government could only be a temporary makeshift. The workers' revolution would have to spread to other areas quickly, or collapse. Over 150 years ago, in the *Communist Manifesto*, Marx and Engels wrote that "united action, of the leading civilised countries at least, is one of the first conditions for the emancipation of the proletariat", and the international intertwining of the forces of production has increased hugely since then, especially in Europe.

We therefore advance, in the first place, a cross-Europe programme, with these main points:

• Tax the rich, Europe-wide.

• Expropriate the banks and the big corporations, Europe-wide. Put them under workers' and democratic control. Gear their resources to the reconstruction of public services, decent jobs, and social welfare.

• Thorough-going democracy across Europe. Social levelling-up across the continent, to the best level of workers' rights and conditions won in any part of it.

• Win workers' governments across Europe, and join them in a democratic federation.

Too extreme? Unrealistic? Leon Trotsky met similar objections in the 1930s. "The masses do not come to us because our ideas are too complicated and our slogans too advanced. It is therefore necessary to simplify our program, water down our slogans — in short, to throw out some ballast".

He responded: "Basically, this means: Our slogans must correspond not to the objective situation, not to the relation of classes, analysed by the Marxist method, but to subjective assessments (extremely superficial and inadequate ones) of what the 'masses' can or cannot accept. But what masses? The mass is not homogeneous. It develops. It feels the pressure of events. It will accept tomorrow what it will not accept today. Our cadres will blaze the trail with increasing success for our ideas and slogans, which will be shown to be correct, because they are confirmed by the march of events and not by subjective and personal assessments".

Trotsky also argued that where the revolutionary socialists were a small minority, they should not limit themselves to reciting their programme and waiting for support to arrive, but should also seek leverage in the debates and battles opened up by the inadequate programmes of bigger forces.

The French and Greek elections, and the Dutch government crisis, which have showed that the capitalist classes' European strategy is in trouble, have also showed that the revolutionary left is still small (1.2% for Antarsya in Greece, 1.8% for NPA and Lutte Ouvrière in France), and that so far the shift to the left is a shift to left social democracy (Syriza in Greece, SP in Netherlands, Mélenchon in France).

In 1934, for example, Trotsky polemicised with his Belgian comrades when they wanted to respond to an economic "labour plan", of a vaguely state-capitalist sort, proposed by the big social-democratic party, just by scorning it.

Trotsky agreed that "it would be more correct to call it: the plan to deceive the toilers". He agreed that, as such, it was only "a new, or a renovated instrument of bourgeois-democratic (or even semi-democratic) conservatism". In fact, the author of the Plan, social-democratic leader Henri de Man, would become a collaborator with the Nazi occupation in World War Two.

Told by his Belgian comrades that "the working masses are absolutely indifferent to the Labor Plan and are in general in a state of depression", Trotsky said he didn't know, but accepted there might well be "a certain nervous exhaustion and passivity of the workers".

Yet he insisted that "our task is twofold", and not just one of expounding and scorning. "First, to explain to the advanced workers the political meaning of the 'plan', that is, decipher the manoeuvres of the social-democracy at all stages; secondly, to show in practice to possibly wider circles of workers that insofar as the bourgeoisie tries to put obstacles to the realisation of the plan we fight hand in hand with the workers to help them make this experiment.

"We share the difficulties of the struggle but not the illusions. Our criticism of the illusions must, however, not increase the passivity of the workers and give it a pseudo-theoretic justification but on the contrary push the workers forward. Under these conditions, the inevitable disappointment with the 'Labor Plan' will not spell the deepening of passivity but, on the contrary, the going over of the workers to the revolutionary road" (emphasis added).

A similar approach had been taken by the German Communist Party in 1921-3, increasing its mass support, and putting it on the brink of a revolutionary situation in October 1923 (which, however, under Stalin's malign guidance from Moscow, the Communist Party then botched).

Rapid inflation in Germany meant that the bosses could, by delaying tax payments, make them nominal. Deprived of revenues, the government had to print money to keep going, which in turn produced more rapid inflation: a vicious circle.

In May 1921 the Social Democrat minister Robert Schmidt proposed "appropriation of real values", or "Sachwerterfassung": the government should tax capital by taking a 20% share in all businesses. That would both help the government guide the shattered economy and bring in real income.

The government never implemented the idea, but it gained popularity in a working class angry that pay-as-you-go taxes on their wages were the only taxes being collected effectively. The Social Democratic-led unions took it up, demanding a 25% share.

In November 1921 the Communist Party decided to pick up on the demand for "appropriation of real values", proposing it at a rate of 51% to allow public control of the economy.

Through to 1923, "Sachwerterfassung" became a major theme of CP advocacy, soon linked with the call for a "workers' government" (a joint Communist-Social Democrat government which would carry out a specified series of radical measures, such as the "appropriation of real values" and workers' control over production).

The left national Keynesian programmes cannot be used for leverage in this way, because trying to do that would pull us into the false position of advocating the rebuilding of barriers between nations as a desirable first step (rather than as a temporary expedient maybe necessary if one national labour movement moves far ahead of others).

We cannot endorse the Euro-Keynesian programmes as a "first step", because they beg the question of how to deal with the banks' resistance; they dodge the issue of "labour-market reform" (in fact, the more mainstream versions openly support "labour movement reform" and cuts in current social spending, arguing only that those cuts should be offset by public investment spending); and in general they are advice to the ruling classes rather than mobilisation plans for the working class.

We can take many elements in the Euro-Keynesian programmes — cancellation of debt (at least partial); increased social spending (at least on investment projects); democratic control of the ECB — and sharpen and build on them.

In that way our criticism will not increase passivity — by suggesting that nothing but a uniform shade of grey is possible until everyone first rallies round the revolutionary socialist minority — but make the most of all the divisions and disputes within the system.

• From *Solidarity* 245, 9 May 2012

Open letter to the left: Do you really want the EU to break up?

Dear comrades,

Do you really want the European Union to break up?
The majority of Greek workers do not. In the 6 May election, 70% voted for parties opposed to the cuts, but polls show that 80% want Greece to stay within the EU and within the euro.

The party that did best in the election, the left coalition Syriza, says that a left government in Greece should refuse the cuts, call the bluff of the EU leaders — who may want cuts, but also want to stop the eurozone breaking up — and enforce a renegotiation.

They want a united Europe without cuts. So do we. If the Greek left wins a majority, and the EU refuses to concede, then we want a workers' government in Greece which will break with EU leaders but not "leave Europe" — which will instead fight to spread workers' rule across Europe.

Yet for decades now most of the British left — and the left in a few other European countries, such as Denmark — has agitated "against the EU". The agitation has suggested, though rarely said openly, we should welcome and promote every pulling-apart of the EU, up to and including the full re-erection of barriers between nation-states.

Now it's not certain that the EU / ECB / IMF troika will dare cut off funds to the Greek government, and force it into "defaulting" on its debt (failing to make payments on the debt when they're due). If Greece defaults, it is not certain that it will quit or be forced out of the euro.

If Greece quits the euro, it's not certain that the exit will set off an unravelling of the whole eurozone. And even if the whole eurozone unravels, the underlying EU structure could remain solid.

An argument can be made — debatable, but not absurd, and not necessarily "anti-EU" — that realistically a Greek government would do better now to negotiate an orderly exit from the euro, rather than to plunge on towards a high probability of forced and chaotic exit.

The economist who has argued most strongly for Greece to negotiate an exit from the euro, Costas Lapavitsas, also insists that he is not calling for Greece to quit the EU.

Yet the possibility of a serious unravelling of the patchwork, bureau-

15

cratic semi-unification of Europe, slowly developed over the last sixty years, is more real today than ever before. The decisive push for unravelling, if it comes, will probably be from the nationalist and populist right.

And that calls the bluff of a whole swathe of the British left.

For decades, most of the British left has been "anti-EU" as a matter of faith. In Britain's 1975 referendum on withdrawing from the EU, almost the whole left, outside Workers' Liberty's forerunner Workers' Fight, campaigned for withdrawal. Since then the left has hesitated explicitly to demand withdrawal. It has limited itself to "no to bosses' Europe" agitation, implying but not spelling out a demand for the EU to be broken up.

The agitation has allowed the left to eat its cake and have it. The left can chime in with populist-nationalist "anti-Europe" feeling, which is stronger in Britain than in any other EU country. It can also cover itself by suggesting that it is not really anti-European, but only dislikes the "bosses'" character of the EU.

As if a confederation of capitalist states could be anything other than capitalist. As if the cross-Europe policy of a collection of neo-liberal governments could be anything other than neo-liberal.

As if the material force behind neo-liberal cuts were the relatively flimsy Brussels bureaucracy, rather than the mighty bureaucratic-military-industrial complexes of member states. As if the answer is to oppose confederation and cross-Europeanism as such, rather than the capitalist, neo-liberal, bureaucratic character of both member states and the EU.

As if the EU is somehow more sharply capitalist, anti-worker, and neo-liberal than the member states. In Britain more than any other country we have seen successive national governments, both Tory and New Labour, repeatedly objecting to EU policy as too soft, too "social", too likely to entrench too many workers' rights.

As if the answer is to pit nations against Europe, rather than workers against bosses and bankers.

When *Socialist Worker*, in a recent Q&A piece, posed itself the question, "wouldn't things be better for workers if Britain pulled out of the EU?", it answered itself with a mumbling "yes, but" rather than a ringing "yes".

"*Socialist Worker* is against Britain being part of a bosses' Europe". Oh? And against Britain being part of a capitalist world, too?

Britain would be better off in outer space? Or walled off from the world North Korea-style? "But withdrawing from the EU wouldn't guarantee workers' rights — the Tories remain committed to attacking us". Indeed. And just as much so as the EU leaders, no?

As recently as 2009, the Socialist Party threw itself into a electoral coalition called No2EU. Every week in its "Where We Stand" it declaims: "No to the bosses' neo-liberal European Union!", though that theme rarely appears in its big headlines.

The RMT rail union, in some ways the most left-wing union in Britain, backed No2EU and today backs the "People's Pledge". This "Pledge" is a campaign to call for parliamentary candidates to demand a referendum on British withdrawal from the EU, and support them only if they agree.

It was initiated by, and is mostly run by, right-wing Tories, but fronted by a Labour leftist, Mark Seddon. It is backed by many Tory MPs — and by some Labour left MPs such as Kelvin Hopkins, John Cryer, and Ronnie Campbell, and by Green MP Caroline Lucas.

The referendum call is a soft-soap demand for British withdrawal, based on the hope that a majority would vote to quit. (In a recent poll, 55% of people agreed with the statement "Britain should remain a full member of the European Union", but 55% also agreed with the statement "Britain should leave the European Union", so...)

Even the demand for withdrawal is a soft-soap, "tactical" gambit. In principle Britain could quit the EU without disrupting much. It could be like Norway, Iceland, Switzerland: pledged to obey all the EU's "Single Market" rules (i.e. all the neo-liberal stuff) though opting out of a say in deciding the rules; exempt from contributing to the EU budget but also opting out from receiving EU structural and regional funds.

That is not what the no-to-EU-ers want. They want Britain completely out. They want all the other member-states out too. A speech by RMT president Alex Gordon featured on the No2EU website spells it out: "Imperialist, supranational bodies such as the EU seek to roll back democratic advances achieved in previous centuries... Progressive forces must respond to this threat by defending and restoring national democracy. Ultimately, national independence is required for democracy to flourish..."

For decades "anti-EU" agitation has been like background music in the left's marketplace — designed to soothe the listeners and make them more receptive to the goods on offer, but not for attentive listening. If the music should be played at all, then it should be turned up now.

But do you really want the EU broken up? What would happen?

The freedom for workers to move across Europe would be lost. "Foreign" workers in each country from other ex-EU states would face disapproval at best.

There would be a big reduction in the productive capacities of the separate states, cut off from broader economic arenas.

Governments and employers in each state would be weaker in capitalist world-market competition, and thus would be pushed towards crude cost-cutting, in the same way that small capitalist businesses, more fragile in competition, use cruder cost-cutting than the bigger employers.

There would be more slumps and depression, in the same way that the raising of economic barriers between states in the 1930s lengthened and deepened the slump then.

Nationalist and far-right forces, already the leaders of anti-EU political discourse everywhere, would be "vindicated" and boosted. Democracy would shrink, not expand. The economically-weaker states in Europe, cut off from the EU aid which has helped them narrow the gap a bit, would suffer worst, and probably some would fall to military dictatorships.

Before long the economic tensions between the different nations competing elbow-to-elbow in Europe's narrow cockpit would lead to war, as they did repeatedly for centuries, and especially in 1914 and 1939.

The left should fight, not to go backwards from the current bureaucratic, neo-liberal European Union, but forward, towards workers' unity across Europe, a democratic United States of Europe, and a socialist United States of Europe.

Comradely, Workers' Liberty

• From *Solidarity* 246, 16 May 2012

The United States of Europe

By Leon Trotsky (written 1915)

The urge toward unifying the European market which, like the effort towards the acquisition of non-European backward lands, is caused by the development of capitalism, runs up against the powerful opposition of the landed and capitalist classes, in whose hands the tariff apparatus joined with that of militarism (without which the former means nothing) constitutes an indispensable weapon for exploitation and enrichment.

The Hungarian financial and industrial bourgeoisie is hostile to economic unification with capitalistically more developed Austria. The Austro-Hungarian bourgeoisie is hostile to the idea of a tariff union with more powerful Germany. On the other hand, the German landowners will never willingly consent to the cancellation of grain duties. Furthermore, the economic interests of the propertied classes of the Central Empires cannot be so easily made to coincide with the interests of the English, French, Russian capitalists and landed gentry. The present war speaks eloquently enough on this score. Lastly, the disharmony and irreconcilability of capitalist interests between the Allies themselves is still more visible than in the Central States.

Under these circumstances, a halfway complete and consistent economic unification of Europe coming from the top by means of an agreement of the capitalist governments is sheer Utopia. Here, the matter can go no further than partial compromises and half-measures. Hence it is that the economic unification of Europe, which offers colossal advantages to producer and consumer alike, and in general to the whole cultural development, becomes the revolutionary task of the European proletariat in its struggle against imperialist protectionism and its instrument — militarism.

The United States of Europe — without monarchies, standing armies and secret diplomacy — is therefore the most important integral part of the proletarian peace program.

The ideologists and politicians of German imperialism frequently came forward, especially at the beginning of the war, with their programme of a European or at least a Central European "United States" (without France and England on the one side and Russia on the other). The program of a violent unification of Europe is just as characteristic of the tendencies of German imperialism as is the tendency of French imperialism whose programme is the forcible dismemberment of Germany.

If the German armies achieved the decisive victory reckoned upon in Germany during the first phase of the war, the German imperialism would have doubtless made the gigantic attempt of realising a compulsory military-tariff union of European states, which would be constructed completely of exemptions, compromises, etc., which would reduce to a minimum the progressive meaning of the unification of the European market.

Needless to say, under such circumstances no talk would be possible of an autonomy of the nations, thus forcibly joined together as the caricature of the European United States. Certain opponents of the program of the United States of Europe have used precisely this perspective as an argument that this idea can, under certain conditions, acquire a "reactionary" monarchist-imperialist content. Yet it is precisely this perspective that provides the most graphic testimony in favour of the revolutionary viability of the slogan of the United States of Europe.

Let us for a moment grant that German militarism succeeds in actually carrying out the compulsory half-union of Europe, just as Prussian militarism once achieved the half-union of Germany, what would then be the central slogan of the European proletariat? Would it be the dissolution of the forced European coalition and the return of all peoples under the roof of isolated national states? Or the restoration of "autonomous" tariffs, "national" currencies, "national" social legislation, and so forth? Certainly not.

The programme of the European revolutionary movement would then be: the destruction of the compulsory anti-democratic form of the coalition, with the preservation and furtherance of its foundations, in the form of complete annihilation of tariff barriers, the unification of legislation, above all of labor laws, etc. In other words, the slogan of the United States of Europe — without monarchies and standing armies — would under the indicated circumstances become the unifying and guiding slogan of the European revolution.

Let us assume the second possibility, namely, an "undecided" issue of the war. At the very beginning of the war, the well-known professor Liszt, an advocate of "United Europe," argued that should the Germans fail to conquer their opponents, the European unification would nevertheless be accomplished, and in Liszt's opinion it would be even more complete than in the case of a German victory.

By the ever growing need of expansion, the European states, hostile to one another but unable to cope with one another, would continue to hinder each other in the execution of their "mission" in the Near East, Africa and Asia, and they would everywhere be forced back by the United States of North America and by Japan. Precisely in case of a stalemate in the war, in Liszt's opinion, the indispensability of an economic and military agreement among the European great powers would come to the fore against weak and backward peoples, but above all, of course, against their own working masses.

We pointed out above the colossal obstacles that lie in the way of realising this programme. Even a partial overcoming of these obstacles would mean the establishment of an imperialist trust of European States, a predatory share-holding association. And this perspective is on occasion adduced unjustifiably as proof of the "danger" of the slogan of The United States of Europe, whereas in reality this is the most graphic proof of its realistic and revolutionary significance.

If the capitalist states of Europe succeeded in merging into an imperialist trust, this would be a step forward as compared with the existing situation, for it would first of all create a unified, all-European material base for the working class movement. The proletariat would in this case have to fight not for the return to "autonomous" national states, but for the conversion of the imperialist state trust into a European Republican Federation.

However... the plan of the imperialist "United States of Europe" has given way to the plans, on the one side, of an economic union of Austria-Germany and on the other side of the quadruple alliance with its war tariffs and duties supplemented with militarism directed against one another. After the foregoing it is needless to enlarge on the great importance which, in the execution of these plans, the policy of the proletariat of both state "trusts" will assume in fighting against the established tariff and military-diplomatic fortifications and for the economic union of Europe.

Now after the so very promising beginning of the Russian revolution, we have every reason to hope that during the course of this present war a powerful revolutionary movement will be launched all over Europe. It is clear that such a movement can succeed and develop and gain victory only as a general European one. Isolated within national borders, it would be doomed to disaster.

Our social-patriots [socialists who advocated "patriotism" and support for the First World War] point to the danger which threatens the Russian revolution from the side of German militarism. This danger is indubitable, but it is not the only one. English, French, Italian militarism is no less a dreadful enemy of the Russian revolution than the Hohenzollern war machine. The salvation of the Russian revolution lies in its propagation all over Europe. Should the revolutionary movement unfold in Germany, the German proletariat would look for and find a revolutionary echo in the "hostile" countries of the west, and if in one of the European countries the proletariat should snatch the power out of the hands of the bourgeoisie, it would be bound, be it only to retain the power, to place it at once at the service of the revolutionary movement in other countries. In other words, the founding of a stable regime of proletarian dictatorship would be conceivable only if it extended throughout Europe, and consequently in the form of a European Republican Federation. The state-unification of Europe, to be achieved neither by force of arms nor by industrial and diplomatic agreements, would in such a case become the unpostponable task of the triumphant revolutionary proletariat.

The United States of Europe is the slogan of the revolutionary epoch into which we have entered. Whatever turn the war operations may take later on, whatever balance-sheet diplomacy may draw out of the present war, and at whatever tempo the revolutionary movement will progress in the near future, the slogan of the United States of Europe will in all cases retain a colossal meaning as the political formula of the struggle of the European proletariat for power.

In this program is expressed the fact that the national state has outlived itself — as a framework for the development of the productive forces, as a basis for the class struggle, and thereby also as a state form of proletarian dictatorship. Our denial of "national defence", as an outlived political programme for the proletariat, ceases to be a purely negative act of ideological-political self-defence, and acquires all its revolutionary content only in the event that over against the conservative defence of the antiquated national fatherland we place the progressive task, namely the creation of a new, higher "fatherland" of the revolution, of republican Europe, whence the proletariat alone will be enabled to revolutionise and to reorganise the whole world.

Herein, incidentally, lies the answer to those who ask dogmatically: "Why the unification of Europe and not of the whole world?" Europe is not only a geographic term, but a certain economic and cultural-historic community. The European revolution does not have to wait for the revelations in Asia and Africa nor even in Australia and America. And yet a completely victorious revolution in Russia or England is unthinkable without a revolution in Germany, and vice versa. The present war is called a world war, but even after the intervention of the United States, it is Europe that is the arena of war. And the revolutionary problems confront first of all the European proletariat.

Of course, the United States of Europe will be only one of the two axes of the world organisation of economy. The United States of America will constitute the other.

The only concrete historical consideration against the slogan of the United States of Europe was formulated by the Swiss Social Democrat as follows: "The unevenness of economic and political development is the unconditional law of capitalism." From this the Social Democrat draws the conclusion that the victory of socialism is possible in one country and that it is needless therefore to make the dictatorship of the proletariat in each isolated state conditional upon the creation of the United States of Europe. That the capitalist development of various countries is uneven is quite incontestable. But this unevenness is itself extremely uneven. The capitalist levels of England, Austria, Germany or France are not the same. But as compared with Africa and Asia all these countries represent capitalist "Europe," which has matured for the socialist revolution. It is profitable and necessary to reiterate the elementary thought that no single country in its struggle has to "wait" for the others, lest the idea of parallel international action be supplanted by the idea of procrastinating international inaction. Without waiting for the others we begin and we continue the struggle on our own national soil in complete certainty that our initiative will provide the impulse for the struggle in other countries; and if this were not so, then it would be hopeless to think – as is borne out both by historical experience and theoretical considerations – that revolutionary Russia, for example, would be able to maintain herself in the face of conservative Europe, or that Socialist Germany could remain isolated in a capitalist world.

To view the perspectives of the social revolution within a national framework is to succumb to the same national narrowness that forms the content of social-patriotism. Vaillant, until the close of his life, regarded France as the chosen country of the social revolution, and precisely in this sense he insisted upon its defence to the end. Lentsch and others, some hypocritically, others sincerely, believed that the defeat of Germany means above all the destruction of the very foundation of the social revolution. Lastly, our Tseretellis and Chernovs who, in our national conditions, have repeated that sorry experiment of French ministerialism, swear that their policy serves the cause of the revolution and therefore has nothing in common with the policy of Guesde and Sembat. Generally speaking, it must not be forgotten that in social-patriotism there is active, in addition to the most vulgar reformism, a national revolutionary messianism, which regards its national state as chosen for introducing to humanity "socialism" or "democracy," be it on the ground of its industrial development or of its democratic form and revolutionary conquests. (If a completely triumphant revolution were actually conceivable within the limits of a single, better prepared nation, this messianism, bound up with the program of national defence, would have its relative historical justification. But in reality, it does not have it.) Defending the national basis of the revolution which such methods as undermine the international connections of the proletariat, really amounts to undermining the revolution, which cannot begin otherwise than on the national basis, but which cannot be completed on that basis in view of the present economic and military-political interdependence of the European states, which has never been so forcefully revealed as in this war. The slogan, the United States of Europe, gives expression to this interdependence, which will directly and immediately set the conditions for the concerted action of the European proletariat in the revolution.

Social-patriotism which is in principle, if not always in fact, the execution of social-reformism to the utmost extent and its adaptation to the imperialist epoch, proposes to us in the present world catastrophe to direct the policy of the proletariat along the lines of the "lesser evil" by joining one of the warring groups. We reject this method. We say that the European war, prepared by the entire preceding course of development, has placed point-blank the fundamental problems of modern capitalist development as a whole; furthermore, that the line of direction to be followed by the international proletariat and its national detachments must not be determined by secondary political and national features nor by problematical advantages of military preponderance of either side (whereby these problematical advantages must be paid for in advance with absolute renunciation of the independent policy of the proletariat), but by the fundamental antagonism existing between the international proletariat and the capitalist regime as a whole.

This is the only principled formulation of the question and, by its very essence, it is socialist-revolutionary in character. It alone provides a theoretical and historical justification for the tactic of revolutionary internationalism.

Denying support to the state — not in the name of a propaganda circle but in the name of the most important class in society — in the period of the greatest catastrophe, internationalism does not simply eschew "sin" passively but affirms that the fate of world development is no longer linked for us with the fate of the national state; more than this, that the latter has become a vise for development and must be overcome, that is, replaced by a higher economic-cultural organisation on a broader foundation. If the problem of socialism were compatible with the framework of the national state, then it would thereby become compatible with national defence. But the problem of socialism confronts us on the imperialist foundation, that is under conditions in which capitalism itself is forced violently to destroy the national-state frameworks it has itself established.

The imperialist half-unification of Europe might be achieved, as we tried to show, as a result of a decisive victory of one group of the great powers as well as a consequence of an inconclusive outcome of the war. In either instance, the unification of Europe would signify the complete trampling underfoot of the principle of self-determination with respect to all weak nations and the preservation and centralisation of all the forces and weapons of European reaction: monarchies, standing armies and secret diplomacy.

The democratic republican unification of Europe, a union really capable of guaranteeing the freedom of national development, is possible only on the road of a revolutionary struggle against militarist, imperialist, dynastic centralism, by means of uprisings in individual countries, with the subsequent merger of these upheavals into a general European revolution. The victorious European revolution, however, no matter how its course in isolated countries may be fashioned can, in consequence of the absence of other revolutionary classes, transfer the power only to the proletariat. Consequently the United States of Europe represents the form – the only conceivable form – of the dictatorship of the European proletariat.

• From the *'Programme of Peace'*, a series of articles published in *Nashe Slovo* (1915-16).

Greece: the fight for workers' control

By Theodora Polenta

In the run-up to Greece's election on 17 June, EU leaders tried to blackmail the Greek people into voting for the pro-cuts parties.

In the end, they forced a very thin parliamentary majority (based on a minority of the votes cast) for New Democracy and Pasok, the two main parties which promised to continue with the "memorandum" imposed by the EU/ ECB/ IMF "troika".

A new government based on a ND-Pasok coalition is unlikely to last long. The potential for winning a left government in Greece committed to refusing the "memorandum" remains high.

From the social democrats came soft blackmailing — "comply, and we can sort out some concessions; but defy, and that means disaster".

That was the soft-cop accompaniment to the hard blackmailing and threats of immediate expulsion of Greece from the eurozone by the mujahedeen of neoliberalism.

Daniel Cohn-Bendit, who was "Danny the Red" in France's May 1968 movement and is now a sort of pink-Green, added himself to the list of those blackmailing the Greek people.

Cohn-Bendit had previously been "pro-Greek", and he switched when a left political alternative in Greece became a possibility. Now he said, as brutally as German finance minister Schäuble or more so, that the eurozone and EU will stop cooperating with Greece — i.e. stop bailing out Greece and push Greece into bankruptcy — if Syriza sticks with its promises to cancel the memorandum and reinstating people's wages to the 2009 level.

From the social democrats, the magic words are Eurobonds for development projects. But even if these come, the major developments proposed are in areas of "low employment intensity":

1. Energy (which will involved further privatisation of the Greek energy sector, more redundancies, and a looting of our collective wealth and infrastructure)

2. Transportation and "big projects" in motorways. Many such projects remain unfinished; now they will be financed by European bonds and pre-

sumably handed to German and French companies

3. Oil pipelines (subject to the resolution of the conflicts and decisions on which pipelines will pass via Greece).

The projects will have a nil impact on improving the majority of the Greek population's living standards and working conditions, as they are not in areas such as industry, agriculture, clothing, food, etc.

With the social-democratic carrot came the stick from the mujahedeen of austerity: Schäuble, Merkel, Barroso, Draghi, Provopoulos, Lagarde.

They equated Syriza getting elected with inevitable Greek exit from the eurozone, with Greek bankruptcy, and with further deterioration of the Greek people living standards and working conditions.

They terrorised the Greek people by pretending that they were fully prepared, with a plethora of plan Bs, Cs and Zs in the event of a Greek euro exit.

Reuters "revealed" that the eurozone finance ministers are preparing plans for a Greek exit. Lagarde and other IMF representatives stated that the IMF is prepared for a Greek exit from the eurozone. Schäuble stated that both ECB and Bundesbank were drawing up contingency plans.

What is on offer from the pro-memorandum parties, Pasok and ND, despite their promises to renegotiate the memorandum, is more of the same: austerity measures and attacks on people's living standards and working conditions.

The economic programme of ND leader Antonis Samaras could be summarised as "memorandum, memorandum and more memorandum". He is very fuzzy and vague about the "social measures" and "social relief that ND is intended to implement and very precise on the anti-working class measures that "need to be implemented".

Despite the deficiencies, the hesitancies, and the reformist character of the programme which Syriza presented for 17 June, it should be applauded when it says clearly that Syriza will scrap the memorandum, restore trade union rights, etc.

Syriza's commitment that not even a single penny should be given to the creditors if the people's needs of decent wages, pensions, welfare state provisions have not been met should be applauded.

Despite the pressure put on Syriza to water down their defiance against the memorandum and come to terms with a renegotiation, it has not surrendered. It has maintained its links with the people and movements that have been actively supporting it.

Syriza leader Alexis Tsipras pledged to immediately remove the Cabinet Act which reduced the minimum wage by 22% (32% for under-25s).

He also pledged to to restore unemployment benefits to previous levels and extend their duration, to restore and extend sickness and maternity, to restore the power of collective bargaining agreements, to cancel the debt of heavily indebted households, to repeal the regressive property tax for the poor working classes.

These policies need the support of each worker, each trade union and neighbouring community movement activist, each unemployed person, each worker in precarious or part-time flexible employment.

Syriza's program can be summarized into three main points:

• people before Greek bond holders and market forces — cancellation of the memorandum;

• write off of most of the debt and freeze interest rates and debt payments for the remaining renegotiated debt

• expansion of democracy and safeguarding of Greece's threatened sovereignty — Troika out of Greece.

The programme has triggered a wave of criticism from different sections of the left.

The criticism varies. Xekinima presents comradely criticism. It advocates a vote for Syriza and support for the formation of a Syriza-led left government, but criticises Syriza for not adopting a full socialist program.

KKE and Antarsya reject Syriza's program as a limited reformist effort far behind the needs of the Greek working class. They declare that Syriza's promise to cancel the memorandum is a hoax and allege that really Syriza is proposing a soft renegotiation of the memorandum.

They say that Syriza's political role is to be a new Pasok to replace the centre-left vacuum and provide a left face for the memorandum politics. They denounce Syriza for its pro-EU stance.

They claim that the left should advocate the cancellation of the debt tied up with an exit from the eurozone, and EU, which should be "anti-capitalist" (for Antarsya) or "under popular power and control" (for KKE).

The problem with these attitudes is not that we can trust Syriza's leaders and be sure they won't buckle under increased pressure (they may), or that we can be sure that Syriza's tactic of calling the bluff of the EU leaders will work (it probably won't).

The trouble is that, under cover of left rhetoric, KKE and Antarsya are declaring defeat in advance. They are giving up on the battle to hold Syriza to its promises, and they are helping the EU and ECB leaders by sparing them the political firestorm they will have to ride through in order to expel Greece from the eurozone.

Syriza has a serious reformist programme which, if implemented, would bring gains for the Greek and European working class.

The "Euro-Keynesian" programme is reformist not because it proposes something impossible but because it is limited and naive about the ferocities of class struggle.

Revolutionary Marxists should point that out. But there is no sense in demanding that Syriza adopt a socialist programme. Syriza is what it is. Demanding it adopt a socialist programme cannot transform it into a revolutionary party. All it can do is, to some degree or another, encourage illusions among workers that a "socialist programme" is no more than the Syriza policy pushed a bit more to the left by pressure.

On the other hand, Antarsya and KKE are abstaining from the class struggle, which at this point has been transferred from the industrial sphere to the political stage. They do this by distancing themselves from Syriza and the prospect of a government of the left — in fact, a version of what the Communist International in its revolutionary period termed an illusory workers' government which could nevertheless become a starting point for a battle to create a real workers' government.

A lot of respectable economists are implicitly backing Syriza's stance. Nobel prize winning economist Paul Krugman put it succinctly the other day when he told Radio Four that "it is deeply destructive to pursue austerity in a depression". Another economist has stated that the worst choice that Greece could follow is the continuation of the memorandum policies, even with an addition of some anaemic growth measures.

A further ten years of austerity would lead the Greek economy into deep stagnation and negative growth and thus inevitably to a Greek bankruptcy, exit from the euro, and possibly the destruction of democracy by a military coup.

Syriza claims that the cost of a potential eurozone breakdown outweighs the cost to EU governments of bailing out Greece and scrapping the memorandum. There is a real basis for this attempt to call the EU leaders' bluff.

The eurozone is ill-placed to resist further disintegration if Greece falls out, and the cost of a euro break-up would be huge (between 10% and 13% of GDP according to the *Financial Times*, 17 May 2012).

There is also a real basis for the EU leaders' attempts to blackmail Greek voters. A Greece expelled from the eurozone would suffer economic chaos even if led by a workers' government.

The eurozone political leaders cannot be trusted to act in an objective or rational way. They could decide to force Greece out of the eurozone, driven that way by the desire to set and example and punish Greece for misbehaving and not sticking to the memorandum. Or they could stumble into it.

It is the political responsibility of Syriza and the revolutionary left to alert and politically prepare the Greek working class for the effects of Greece being forced out of the eurozone.

The key issues then will be the development of European working-class solidarity; comprehensive workers' control in Greece, including over the distribution of food and other essentials; and the development of workers' self-defence groups to deal with the threat of the Golden Dawn fascists and of a possible future military coup.

• Abridged and reworked from *Solidarity* 248, 6 June 2012

Who are the Greek left?

In the Greek left, the Syriza coalition and the KKE are the biggest groups, but there are many others. This briefing describes the background to Syriza and KKE, and to some of the groups in Greece which consider themselves Trotskyist.

Syriza

Syriza is an alliance of 13 left parties and groups. The dominant force in it is Synaspismos. It was formed in 2004 (with only five groups in the alliance then).

It campaigns now, and campaigned in the run-up to 6 May, for a left-unity government. After 6 May it proposed six points to other parties after 6 May as conditions for Syriza's participation in a coalition government:

• Reverse all the anti-working-class policies implemented during the last two years — wage and pension reductions and abolition of collective bargaining agreements, union rights etc

• Freeze all debt payments. A moratorium on the debt for at least three years.

• Nationalisation of the banks under workers' control.

• Elect a committee to examine and assess the Greek debt and write off the "illegal" part of the debt

• Introduce proportional representation

• Scrap protection for MPs from being prosecuted for acts of corruption and robbery of public money.

It wants Greece to stay in the EU and eurozone, and argues that defiant rejection of the cuts imposed on Greece by the EU, ECB, and IMF can force the EU leaders to back down.

Synaspismos

Synaspismos essentially comes out of the "Interior" ("Eurocommunist") faction of the old Communist Party of Greece, KKE.

In 1987 the two factions of the KKE formed an electoral coalition under the name Synaspismos. In 1989-90 Synaspismos joined a coalition government with New Democracy (Tories), theoretically on a short-term mandate to clean up corruption.

Most Synaspismos members and leaders came to think that the coalition was a bad move. The collapse of the USSR in 1991 led to KKE-Exterior quitting the Synaspismos coalition, and the remainder of Synaspismos converting itself from a coalition to a party.

"Eurocommunism" was a trend in many Communist Parties in the 1970s to distance themselves from the USSR and Stalinism and to open up to movements like feminism.

In Britain the "Eurocommunists" soon became, essentially, right-wing Labourites or liberals with a top-coating of Marxist jargon. In some countries, including Greece, the "Eurocommunists" were more left-wing.

The KKE-Interior was so called because led by those "inside" Greece (rather than in exile) under the military dictatorship of 1967-74.

Some of the old "Eurocommunist" leaders, such as Fotis Kouvelis, split off from Synaspismos in June 2010 to form the Democratic Left. Most Synaspismos members today have joined since the days of "Eurocommunism".

The Synaspismos youth movement is more left-wing than the older members, and among the older members too there are several different shades of politics.

KKE

The Communist Party of Greece (KKE) is the oldest political party in Greece, and has much deeper roots in Greek working-class history than Pasok (founded only in 1974, and without the organic links with trade unions which the Labour Party has in Britain). This makes the landscape of the left in Greece very different from in Britain.

KKE was founded in 1918, when the workers' revolution in Russia inspired a number of small socialist groups to join together and many workers to join them.

The first general secretary of the KKE, Pantelis Pouliopoulos, and others, stayed loyal to revolutionary Marxism and became Trotskyists, but the majority of the KKE became Stalinised.

Between 1941 and 1944 the KKE played a big role in the armed resistance to the Nazi occupation of Greece. A civil war followed, between 1946 and 1949, between KKE-led forces and the forces of the monarchy, backed by British troops and the USA.

The KKE of today is the diehard-Stalinist remnant of the old KKE, after the splintering-way of "Eurocommunist" currents which have flowed into Syriza and of Maoist groups,

It proposes a "popular government" which will "disengage from the EU" and overthrow "the monopolies" at some time in the future, but all large measures have to wait for that distant future. For now it has no answers but to strengthen the KKE so that it can pursue "the path of rupture, conflict, [which] requires sacrifices". The KKE is diehard-Stalinist, and publicly mourned North Korean dictator Kim Jong-il.

Xekinima

Xekinima was in Syriza between 2008 and 2011. It quit last year but called for a vote for Syriza or other left parties on 6 May, and backed Syriza's call for a united left government.

"Xekinima urges Syriza to make a bold call to the rank and file of the KKE and other left forces to join in an electoral bloc on an anti-austerity platform and to fight for a majority left government with a socialist programme".

The tag "with a socialist programme" reflects Xekinima's links with the Socialist Party in England, which for a long time summed up its aim as "Labour to power with a socialist programme", as if a full socialist programme were something that could be achieved by nudging along Labour (or Syriza).

Xekinima's attitude to Europe is, however, very different from the "No2EU" Socialist Party's.

"While the vast majority of Greeks vociferously oppose the austerity programme they also want to remain in the eurozone. They understandably fear the aftermath of exiting the common currency".

DEA

DEA is a group within Syriza which sees itself as part of the same "tradition" as the SWP in Britain. Its international links are, however, not with the SWP, but with the ISO in the USA, which the SWP expelled from its international network in 2001 in an obscure dispute, and Socialist Alternative in Australia.

DEA commented on the 6 May election: "we commit ourselves once again to doing anything we can to keep Syriza moving in a radical left-wing direction..."

It further explains: "In the Syriza alliance, we are trying to organise around the slogan: 'Not a single sacrifice for the euro, no illusions in the drachma'. Our goal is a left-wing policy that confronts the vulgar 'Europeanism' which legitimises austerity policies today, but without taking responsibility for raising a call for an immediate return to the drachma... If [a return to the drachma] does happen under the current constellation of social and political forces, the results will be bitter for the Greek people..."

Kokkino

Kokkino is a splinter from DEA, also within Syriza. It appears more ecumenical than DEA. It declares that a left government will "face a coordinated attack from the markets" and should respond with measures like "stopping payments, nationalisation with compensation of banks and key sectors of the economy, control of trade and capital flows... The key is to organise a wide support network for a left government by the organisation and mobilisation of its social base".

Democratic Left

The Democratic Left is a split from Synaspismos in 2011. Although it voted against the second EU/ ECB/ IMF "memorandum", in negotiations after 6 May it indicated it would cooperate in a government carrying through the "memorandum".

Antarsya, SEK, Spartakos

Antarsya is a coalition of ten left groups including two Trotskyist currents, the SEK and OKDE-Spartakos, Maoist groups, and splinters from the KKE tradition.

It got 1.2% of the vote in the 6 May election, with the slogan "Bread, Education, Freedom" (clunkily adapted from the Bolsheviks' "Bread, Land, and Peace" in 1917: the Bolsheviks also pushed less bland demands for workers' control, for the organisation of the working class, for Red Guards, and for power to workers' councils).

The vote was more than in 2009, but has disappointed Antarsya activists and led to some debate between them.

DEA criticises Antarsya as follows: "Antarsya... adapted the slogan 'an anti-capitalist exit from the euro'. This formulation isn't honest... If we are talking about an anti-capitalist overthrow of the existing system and the new system that would emerge from this, then a slogan about currency isn't the best place to start... For most of the comrades of Antarsya, the way to resolve the contradiction in their everyday political activity is to forget about the adjective 'anti-capitalist' and speak only about an exit from the euro, pure and simple..."

SEK, however, praises this position of Antarsya for bringing EU withdrawal into *immediate* left politics. The KKE is very anti-EU, but talks about Greek withdrawal from the EU as something which should happen only with a "popular" (KKE-backed) government already in power in Greece, not *now*.

SEK does not oppose the call for a united left government, but stresses the "limits" and sees the answer in more militancy in workplaces.

SEK is the group "officially" linked to the SWP in Britain. OKDE-Spartakos is linked with the "Mandelite" current represented by such organisations as the NPA in France. (There is a tiny affiliate of this current in Britain, called Socialist Resistance).

Spartakos suggests that the left should give "extra-parliamentary support or votes in parliament to all measures of a leftist government that break with the politics of capital", but emphasises struggle for "workers' control and workers' self-management".

EEK, OKDE

There are two main Trotskyist groups which stood in the 6 May elections against both Syriza and Antarsya.

EEK (which got 0.08%) was historically linked to the "Healyite" SLL/WRP in Britain, which was the biggest and most visible revolutionary left group in Britain in the 1960s and early 70s. EEK stuck with the WRP even after it went crazy (from about 1968) and then (from 1976) took money from the Libyan and Iraqi governments to sustain itself, and in return praised those tyrannies. In 1987 Healy expelled the EEK because it would not go along with his applause for Gorbachev. EEK is now linked not with other ex-Healyite groups but with Politica Obrera in Argentina. It declares:

"Elections will not provide the solution, the solution lies in the immediate organisation and victorious conduct of an indefinite General Political Strike that will last until the fall of the Papademos government and its potential successors... a red socialist Greece in a red socialist Europe".

OKDE (which got 0.02%) is the result of a split from OKDE-Spartakos by young activists who saw the whole "Mandelite" current as drifting into soft, flabby politics. The OKDE comrades are open and keen to discuss, and Workers' Liberty has attended meetings with them and carried comment from them in *Solidarity*.

OKDE's view on the EU is different from ours. OKDE distinguishes itself on the Greek left by raging against the EU as "the anti-worker headquarters, the prison of peoples".

OKDE calls for a revolutionary party and a socialist revolution, but also for a Constituent Assembly.

KKEML, MLKKE

There are many Maoist groups in Greece, offshoots of the strength of the KKE tradition. Two of them, KKE-ML and ML-KKE, have formed an electoral alliance focused on "the struggle of our people for leaving the EU and NATO and to overthrow the domination of imperialism". It won 0.25% on 6 May.

• From *Solidarity* 247, 23 May 2012

What is capitalist crisis?

By Colin Foster

The capitalist system not only exploits workers. It also ruins capitalists, through periodic crises. Why?

The driving force of capitalism is the self-expansion of capital: a spiral circuit that transforms money-wealth into labour-power and means of production, then into production, then into new commodities, then, through sale, into more money-wealth. Why should that circuit be broken, so that money-wealth, workers, factories, and unsold stocks all lie idle?

According to an old law of orthodox economics, Say's Law, such general crises are impossible in a pure free-market capitalist system. Minor excesses, maladjustments, and disproportions are certainly possible, but, given the chance, market mechanisms will restore balance before any general crisis can develop. General crises must therefore result from impurities in the system which clog up the mechanisms of the market.

For example: in a crisis, workers are unemployed. No capitalist finds sufficient profit in employing them. Say's Law backs up the commonplace argument that trade unions, or minimum-wage laws, must be "pricing the workers out of jobs", by preventing wage rates from falling low enough to make employing those workers profitable.

Say's Law

Another way to put Say's Law is this: if capitalists operate the given means of production and workforce at full capacity, then they will automatically find buyers for all they produce, minor miscalculations and maladjustments aside.

Suppose a capitalist brings goods worth £200 to sell on market-day, Saturday. The £200, the total price of output, is exactly equal to the total of incomes flowing from that business. If the wages bill is £80, say, and the capitalist pays £60 to his landlord, then the capitalist's expected profit is £200 less £80 less £60. Or, £200, the total price of output, is equal to the wages (£80), plus the rent and interest (£60), plus the profit (£60).

The capitalist will already have paid out the wages, rent, and interest — on Friday, maybe. He can also get credit from the bank to the amount of his expected profit. So, at the same time as he arrives in the market-place with supply worth £200, he, his workers, and his landlord arrive there with demand totalling £200.

Of course an individual capitalist may miscalculate and produce unwanted goods. Then he will have to sell his products at less than the expected profit, while some other capitalist, making more wanted goods, will make more than the expected profit. Capital will shift from the unwanted line of production to the wanted one, in a constantly self-correcting process.

A first objection: is there enough money?

An apparently unjustified assumption has been slipped in to the argument. Where does the capitalist get cash from to pay wages, rent and interest? Why assume that he can get credit from the bank to the amount of his expected profit? In short: there is no effective demand for any capitalist's goods unless the buyers have cash in hand, and where do they get the cash from?

In fact, however, there is plenty of cash on hand. As soon as "credit money" — bank notes and cheques — is developed, banks and governments can multiply the amount of money available very easily. In Britain in 2012, the total of money in cash and bank accounts is about £1300 billion. Output was about £30 billion a week, so full-employment output might be about £33 billion. There was plenty of money to buy the output. If the money available were the only limit, demand could go up to £1300 billion a week (or more: a £10 note which passes from hand to hand once a day can serve for £70 of demand in a week, not just £10).

Claims that "there is not enough money" to pay for better health care, schools, housing, or public transport are always nonsense. Under capitalism, relations between people — who produces what, how, for whom? — are always expressed through relations between things, between different commodities and money. The claim that "there is not enough money" for social purposes uses the money-expression of human realities to conceal those realities.

Some social goals, of course, cannot be afforded, because of lack of productive resources or because of their ecological cost. But there is plenty of money. There is plenty of money — only that money, or, to get to the root of it, the social power represented by the large accumulations of money, is in the hands of those who will not use it for social purposes.

A second objection: will the money be spent?

Full-employment output in Britain would be about £33 billion a week, and the money on hand is about £1300 billion. Then why should the portion of that money which people spend each week — i.e. circulate from hand to hand — be £33 billion rather than £15 billion or £60 billion?

Say's Law assumes that the workers, the capitalists, and the landlords spend each week what they get in income that week. In other words, it assumes that money is only a means of exchange, a technical trick for making quicker and easier the barter of one bundle of commodities for another.

People want money only as a means for getting the commodities they want.

In an idealised economy of independent producers in small farms and workshops, with no wage labour, that might be true. Under capitalism it is very far from true.

The drive of the capitalist is to transform money into more money. The other commodities — machines, buildings, labour-power, products — are only means to that end. Rather than wanting money as a means to get commodities, the capitalist wants commodities as a means to get money.

Money is not just a technical device. It is a store of value, a representation of command over human labour.

Money can always be transformed into commodities. Commodities cannot always be transformed into money.

Thus people may well circulate only, say, an average of £30 billion a week. If they do this at a time when production has been running at full employment (£33 billion a week), then unsold stocks will increase. After a period of increasing unsold stocks, the capitalists will cut production to £30 billion a week, restoring balance between supply and effective demand but at less than full employment.

This objection to Say's Law is fundamental. It shows that crises are rooted in the way that capitalism gives power over human relations to the alienated, mystified expression of those relations in money-relations.

Crises are generated by the whole circuit of capital, not just by capitalist production

Crises, in other words, are based on the role of money in capitalist society. They result from — indeed, they are — disturbances in the flow from money-capital to means-of-production and labour-power to products to money again.

As Marx put it: "The real crisis can only be educed from the real movement of capitalist production, competition and credit" [*Theories of Surplus Value* vol.2 (*TSV2*)].

But this shows that some Marxistic theories of crises are inadequate.

One inadequate theory deduces crises directly from "underconsumption" — from the fact that workers consume relatively little of what they produce. Therefore (so it is argued) the capitalists can never have an adequate market for what they produce.

"Underconsumption" does, I think, play a part in the explanation of crises — but it does not explain them directly. It cannot. If it did, then crises would be explained directly from the structure of productive capital — i.e. from the relatively small part in it of "variable capital", capital laid out as wages — without reference to the whole circuit of capital.

Capitalists can have an adequate market for what they produce even if wages are very low. Demand by capitalists and their hangers-on for new machinery, equipment, materials, and luxuries can make up the market.

In any case, what does "under"-consumption mean here? Under what? Low living standards for workers, alongside vast luxury for capitalists, make us angry, but do they necessarily cause trouble for capitalism? How small does the workers' share in what's produced have to be in order to cause crisis? 50 per cent? 20 per cent? Why?

Marx summed up on "underconsumption" as follows: "As matters stand, the replacement of the capital invested in production depends largely upon the consuming power of the non-producing classes... The ultimate reason for all real crises always remains the poverty and restricted consumption of the masses as opposed to the drive of capitalist production to develop the productive forces as though only the absolute consuming power of society constituted their limit". But: "It is pure tautology to say that crises are provoked by a lack of effective demand or effective consumption. The capitalist system does not recognise any forms of consumer other than those who can pay... The fact that commodities are unsaleable means no more than that no effective buyers have been found for them...

"If the attempt is made to give this tautology the semblance of greater profundity, by the statement that the working class receives too small a portion of its own product, and that the evil would be remedied if it received a bigger share, i.e. if its wages rose, we need only note that crises are always prepared by a period in which wages generally rise, and the working class actually does receive a greater share in the part of the annual product destined for consumption...

"It thus appears that capitalist production involves certain conditions independent of people's good or bad intentions, which permit the relative prosperity of the working class only temporarily, and moreover always as a harbinger of crisis" (*Capital vol.2*).

Key elements in crises: capital in movement, and class structure

To get a more adequate theory of crises, we have to follow the argument further.

The possibility of crisis arises from the fact that in capitalism money is not just a means to get goods and services. On the contrary, for the capitalist, money is a means to get more money. Thus money-wealth may be stacked up on one side, and unsold goods and services on the other.

This possibility, however, does not always become reality, at least not on the scale that causes crises. "It is not probable", wrote David Ricardo, "that [anyone] will continually produce a commodity for which there is no demand" (quoted, *TSV2*). There is a balancing mechanism. If supply begins to outrun demand, and unsold commodities begin to stack up, then prices will fall. Commodities become cheaper, and so more attractive. Demand increases. Balance is restored.

In the long term this is true. As Marx sarcastically commented on Ricardo's argument that "continual" overproduction was improbable, "the point in question here is not eternal life" (*TSV2*). "The excess of commodities is always relative; in other words it is an excess at particular prices" (*TSV*). "When Adam Smith explains the fall in the rate of profit from an over-abundance of capital... he is speaking of a permanent effect and this is wrong. As against this, the transitory over-abundance of capital, overproduction and crises are something different. Permanent crises do not exist" (*TSV2*).

There is indeed a balancing mechanism. The problem is that it does not always restore balance smoothly, by continual tiny adjustments, like a thermostat or a governor on an engine. Balance is sometimes restored only jerkily, after convulsions. Why?

Balance could be restored smoothly if society were a single community adjusting its consumption and production against each other — so that any general unexpected "excess" of goods would quickly be cleared just by improving average living standards — and if the question were only one of balancing today's consumption and today's production. But neither assumption holds true for capitalism.

Today's wages and employment are held down — for the sake of tomorrow's profit of individual employers — when from the point of view of the capitalist class as a whole it should make sense to employ more workers, on higher wages, and thus create a market for otherwise unsold goods. And: "The circulation process of capital is not completed in one day but extends over a fairly long period... and great upheavals and changes take place in the market in the course of this period" (*TSV2*). Prior decisions can prevent smooth balancing. The capitalists cannot reduce the cost-price of the machines they have already installed, or the amount of the debts they have already run up. Thus, they may not be able to deal with a disturbance by smoothly reducing the price of their products. They may have to go bust, or hold on to their stocks at a higher price and wait, instead.

Decisions based on future prospects can also undermine smooth balancing today. Capitalists buy new machines not on the basis of weighing their utility against their price, but on the basis of an assessment of how quickly and copiously the money put into the machines can be transformed into more money got by selling the products. If the prospects for getting more money look grim, then the capitalists may not want to buy the new machines (or may not be able to get credit from their bankers in order to buy them), however much the machines' price is reduced.

The decisions about buying new machines and materials are taken by the capitalists, by a different class. "Nothing is more absurd as a means of denying crises, than the assertion that the consumers (buyers) and producers (sellers) are identical in capitalist production. They are entirely distinct categories... [The workers] are... producers without being consumers... in relation to all articles which have to be consumed not individually but industrially... On the other hand, it is equally wrong to say that the con-

39

sumers are producers. The landlord does not produce... and yet he consumes. The same applies to all moneyed interests".

To put it another way: the workers can get work and wages — i.e. they can consume — only if they produce profits, i.e. only if they produce more then they consume, and therefore only if another class or classes (the capitalists and other wealthy classes) provide demand for that surplus production. Or yet another way: "underconsumption" is significant in crises, inasmuch as it means that the burden of balancing consumption and production cannot be borne by workers' consumption but has to be borne by the altogether more erratic demand of the wealthy classes, mainly for investment goods.

A disturbance may expand before balancing out. If an excess is produced, the capitalists cut prices — but they also cut wages, slash jobs, and cancel investment plans, thus depressing demand by far more than can be compensated for by any cut in prices which is less than ruinous in relation to the capitalists' previously-fixed cost-prices and debts. Balance comes only after ruin.

The rate of interest

There is another mechanism to balance the economy through "price" movements, namely, the movements of a special "price", the rate of interest. According to some economists, an ideal free-market capitalist economy could be balanced by the rate of interest moving down when investment (capitalists' purchases of means-of-production) dropped. The fall in the rate of interest makes it cheaper for industrial capitalists to borrow and buy new machinery, and it makes it less attractive for the wealthy to hold their wealth as cash, yielding interest, rather than putting it into industry.

This might work if the movements of the rate of interest were what orthodox economics describes them as — indices of the community adjusting its balance between current consumption and provision for the future. In class-divided capitalist society, they are not that. The rate of interest reflects not some community consensus on the balance between present and future, but a factor in the balance of power between money-capitalists and industrialists.

In a crisis bankers are powerful. The worse-off industrialists are desperate to get credit in order to survive. The rate of interest does not fall. It rises, or remains high. "When businessmen and their bankers begin to scramble for liquidity, both trade credit and bank credit will decline... interest rates for a time rise sharply" (from A F Burns's summary, "Business Cycles", in the *International Encyclopaedia of the Social Sciences*). Or: "This is the period during which moneyed interest enriches itself at the cost of industrial interest" (*TSV2*).

One of Keynes's great contributions was to demolish the argument about the rate of interest automatically putting capitalism into balance. "Our social and business organisation", he wrote, "separates financial provision for the future from physical provision for the future". A Marxist would add: the "provision for the future", financial or physical, is never correlated to future needs, but to immediate prospects of gain.

"The multiplier"

Thus capitalism does not restore its balance automatically and smoothly after slight disturbances. On the contrary, it can magnify those disturbances.

Suppose there is a glut of cloth, for example, because of some disturbance. The cloth-producers cannot sell their wares. Then they cannot pay the suppliers from whom they got materials and equipment on credit, and they, in turn, do not pay their creditors. Workers are laid off, and so the whole market shrinks. The capitalists see this and cancel or postpone investments. The machine-making industries slump; they lay off yet more workers; and the economy spirals downwards. "On the one hand there is a superabundance of all kinds of unsold commodities on the market. On the other hand bankrupt capitalists and destitute, starving workers" (*TSV2*). It seems that no-one has cash. The notes and coins available circulate more slowly, and are augmented by credit less. Keynes called this process "the multiplier".

How disturbances are produced

The argument so far shows that a capitalist economy cannot balance itself automatically, and that disturbances can escalate to the point where a new balance can be reached only after widespread ruin.

Where do the disturbances come from? They may come from outside the core mechanisms of capitalism — from natural disaster or political crisis. If that were all, capitalist crises might be severe, but they would be completely erratic. In fact, they are erratic, but not completely so. There is a definite boom/slump cycle, even though it is irregular and unpredictable in detail.

The core mechanisms of capitalism tend to produce regular major disturbances, in addition to any "external" ones. They do that because production and the market are correlated not by any deliberate plan, but by the movement of money through the circuit of capital, which has its own blind logic. The correlation regularly, chronically, lurches out of balance.

Suppose capitalism is booming. Wages will rise slowly, profits will rise faster. As they see profits rising, capitalists hurry to seize the time by expanding and buying new equipment. Credit (or, to look at the same thing from the other side, debt) expands.

After time, the rate of industrial profit sinks because of the bigger share taken by high finance (as credit is strained), and because, once full-capacity production and full employment are reached, labour costs rise. Some of the "frenetic speculations" and "outright swindles" collapse. Other capitalists, having completed their re-equipment decisions, or seeing the boom slackening, try to slow down in a measured way, cancelling or postponing new investments. The investment-goods industries suffer a collapse in demand. Their difficulties spread to the whole economy, through the "multiplier". Credit dries up. Ruin reigns.

Wages are pushed down, but the lower wages do not — contrary to what one might think from supply-and-demand theory abstracted from the class divisions of capitalism — lead to workers being taken back off the dole queue into jobs. "The pressure of the unemployed compels those who are employed to furnish more labour, and therefore makes the supply of labour to a certain extent independent of the supply of workers. The movement of the law of supply and demand of labour on this basis completes the despotism of capital... The condemnation of one part of the working class to enforced idleness by the overwork of the other part, and vice versa, becomes a means of enriching the individual capitalists..." (*Capital vol.1*).

All this, however, gradually restores profit-rates for the more solid capitalists who have survived. Excess stocks are cleared or written off. Credit eases. A new boom begins.

The length of the cycle is roughly equal to the average lifetime of industrial machinery. "The cycle of related turnovers, extending over a number of years, within which the capital is confined by its fixed component, is one of the material foundations for the periodic cycle in which business passes through successive periods of stagnation, moderate activity, over-excitement and crisis" (*Capital vol.2*).

Marx explains further. As a boom encourages capitalists to undertake big projects railway-building is his example — "labour-power, means of subsistence for this labour-power, fixed capital.. and production materials, are all withdrawn from the market, and an equivalent in money is cast into the market to replace them with; but no product is cast into the market during the year in question to replace the material elements of productive capital withdrawn from it.

"If we were to consider a communist society in place of a capitalist one, then money capital would immediately be done away with, and so too the disguises that transactions acquire through it. The matter would simply be reduced to the fact that the society must reckon in advance how much labour, means of production and means of subsistence it can spend [on such projects]...

"In capitalist society, on the other hand, where any kind of social rationality asserts itself only post festum, major disturbances can and must occur constantly... [As big investment projects boom] the money market is under pressure... prices rise, both for the means of subsistence and for the material elements of production. During this time, too, there are regular business swindles, and great transfers of capital. A band of speculators, contractors, engineers, lawyers etc. enrich themselves. These exert a strong consumer demand on the market, and wages rise as well...

"A part of the reserve army of workers whose pressure keeps wages down is absorbed. Wages generally rise... This lasts until, with the inevitable crash, the reserve army of workers is again released and wages are pressed down once more to their minimum and below it..." (*Capital vol.2*).

Crises are unpredictable

A broad pattern exists. But in detail crises are unpredictable and erratic. They do not arise directly from capitalist production, narrowly defined, but from the whole circuit of capital, which include all the complexities of capitalist finance. They arise from the fact that "market and production are two independent factors" (*TSV2*) — each determined by different people, on different criteria, and on different time-scales, and determined blindly, without any concerted plan. Tiny disturbances can grow into big ones; bigger disturbances can fade away. Any one of a number of disturbances can start the "crisis" phase of a boom/slump cycle: a credit squeeze, a major bankruptcy, the collapse of a major swindle... The details are always complex and always partly accidental.

It is possible for crises to be set off by purely financial disturbances. However, financial problems alone are not generally the cause of crises. Marx roundly denied that stock market crashes would necessarily cause industrial slumps. "As regards the fall in the purely nominal capital, State bonds, shares etc. — in so far as it does not lead to the bankruptcy of the state or of the share company, or to the complete stoppage of reproduction through undermining the credit of the industrial capitalists who hold such securities — it amounts only to the transfer of wealth from one hand to another and will, on the whole, act favourably upon reproduction, since the parvenus into whose hands these stocks or shares fall cheaply are mostly more enterprising than their former owners" (*TSV2*).

Marx's argument is a bit too sweeping, and wrong in detail — stock market crashes tend to ruin "parvenus" more than wealthy Establishment people — but basically he is right. Conversely, stock market booms do not — despite what is often argued, including by some Marxists — "divert" wealth from productive capitalism into "speculation". Stock market booms are favourable circumstances for productive capitalists to scoop together scattered small savings into amounts big enough to function as new productive capitals.

In populistic arguments, money-capitalists are often targetted as the evil makers of crisis, in contrast to the solid plodders of industrial capital. This is false. Crisis is a product of the whole circuit of capital.

The world market and crises

Capitalism is not a single unit, but national economies linked by a world market. This creates factors of instability in addition to those already mentioned.

In a national economy, a government or a central bank can ease crises by measures to ease credit, put more money into circulation, cut taxes, or raise public spending. "Keynesian" policy made such measures into a system, which cannot abolish capitalist crises but which can ease them, if applied intelligently and not offset by international factors. According to Marx, for example, the British crisis of 1847 was eased by the Government suspending the Bank Act, a law which limited the Bank of England's issue of bank notes (*Capital vol.3*).

In the world market, there is no world market or world central bank. If, today, the people and the corporations who hold large amounts of what serves as fallback "world money" — American dollars — drastically lost confidence in the dollar and started a dollar-selling panic, then world "liquidity" would collapse. International trade and investment would be paralysed by shortage of anything to act as cash. The world would probably go back to something like the situation of the 1930s, where world trade shrank drastically and was increasingly confined to shut-off trading blocs centred round major currencies and powers (dollar, pound sterling, franc and so on).

Short of such catastrophe, and even when there is no real world crisis, the workings of the world market can also generate depression in national economies. The capitalist world economy has a tendency towards "uneven development", the weak national economies becoming weaker and the strong national economies stronger. Other tendencies partly counter this one — the very strongest national economies, for example, like the US after World War Two, tend to "overstretch" themselves and slow down — but only partly.

Weaker national economies suffer a chronic "flight of capital" to stronger economies with better infrastructure and more buoyant and secure markets. If they manage to get a boom underway, then orders for imports of investment goods expand rapidly. The underdeveloped national economy cannot produce those machines and equipment itself.

Those imports have to be paid for in dollars. US capitalists can pay for imports in their own currency, but Third World capitalists cannot pay for their imports from the US, Japan, or Germany in pesos, rupees, or dinars. The country's foreign debt spirals. The import orders have to be cancelled and the boom stalled. No boom ever acquires enough upswing to develop a strong infrastructure and buoyant markets and draw capital into the country.

Some Third World countries are chronically in this trap. Despite Marx's comment that "permanent crises do not exist", there are in more or less permanent depression.

Crises and imperialism: "underconsumptionism"
Marxist debate on imperialism has oscillated between approaches start-

ing from the structure of the world economy, and those starting from a drive inside the typical advanced national economy. Some, though not all, of the writers with the second approach have seen imperialism as a way by which this typical advanced national economy deals with its impulses towards crisis. The theory of imperialism is thus made part of the theory of crisis.

I think that is wrong. But analysis of imperialism based on examining the structure of the world economy can help explain crises.

From as early as 1884, on and off, Karl Kautsky explained imperialism as a product of "underconsumption". The poverty of the working class restricted home markets, and thus restricted profitable openings for investment at home; therefore the capitalists were driven to invest and seek markets abroad.

In 1884, he argued that "commodity production yielded a surplus that neither the worker nor the capitalist could consume [because the worker was kept poor and the capitalist could only consume so many luxuries]... Consequently, colonial territories were important for the industrial nations as a market for surplus production" [Dick Geary, *Karl Kautsky*].

But "overproduction" is not a permanent condition; capitalism constantly sheds overproduction through crises and then builds it up again. The idea of a permanent glut of capital compelling a flow abroad is misleading.

A glut compelling a flow abroad would have to be not so much a glut of capital in general as a glut of capital in money-form seeking productive investment. The relation between the supply and demand for such money-capital is determined by the tempo of self-expansion of capital. It is a relation between the profits accumulated from past capitalist exploitation, and the profits available from present capitalist exploitation. The spasmodic nature of capitalist development means that this supply-and-demand relation is constantly falling out of balance.

Regularly capitalism generates "surpluses" of money-capital. But those surpluses are a function of the cycle of boom and slump, not of any absolute level at which an economy becomes "full up" of capital. Indeed, each "surplus" of capital — that is, each crisis — will, unless the working class can seize the opportunity to overthrow capitalism, create the conditions for a lively demand for capital to reappear. Poor countries are likely to have poor capital markets, but they can have surpluses of capital like rich ones.

Besides, there is no reason to suppose that British capitalists, for example, will exhaust all possibilities for investing in Britain before they start investing abroad. In the period before the First World War, British overseas investment tended to be high when domestic investment was high and low when it was low, rather than vice versa [Lance E Davis and Robert A Huttenback, *Mammon and the Pursuit of Empire*].

The notion of an absolute level at which a capitalist economy will become "full up" with capital, so that thereafter it is permanently awash with sur-

45

plus capital, is a recurrent theme in mainstream economics, from Adam Smith to Keynes. It has been attractive to socialists because it seems to show that capitalism must inevitably break down. It is misleading.

Rosa Luxemburg, in her book *The Accumulation of Capital*, developed a different picture of imperialism as driven by "underconsumption".

Luxemburg openly criticised cruder versions of underconsumptionism"; but she posed a puzzle arising from Marx's "schemes of reproduction" (input-output tables for the economy). Where, Luxemburg asked, did the money come from to enable the capitalists to sell the goods in which surplus-value was embodied? Or, rather, where did the "effective demand" come from?

The answer, in fact, is that the government prints the money and the effective demand is generated — erratically, with ups and downs of crisis — by the capitalists' drive to accumulate. But Luxemburg disagreed. Within a pure capitalist economy, she insisted, there was no answer. To survive, capitalism needed non-capitalist consumers. But, as capitalism expanded across the world, the number of non-capitalist consumers decreased. Capitalism would run into bigger and bigger problems, and eventually collapse.

This theory is untenable. Non-capitalist consumers do not help the problem. Where do they get the money from? Non-capitalist consumers do not supply liquidity for capitalism; capitalism supplies liquidity for them.

But the linking of imperialism to "underconsumptionist" crisis remained influential among Marxists, and help disorient many people when they grappled with the unexpected developments of capitalism after the Second World War. Michael Kidron and John Strachey for example saw "the end of imperialism". Since arms spending (Kidron) or welfare spending (Strachey) was draining away the glut of capital, the basic economic mechanism of imperialism no longer operated.

In more revolutionary circles, the idea of the permanent "glut of capital" led to the conclusion that decolonisation would mean metropolitan capitalism choking to death on its uninvestible riches. Even a limited setback to metropolitan capitalism's ability to drain its surplus capital into the colonies would leave it suffocating. Thus the Second World Congress of the Fourth International argued that the loss of colonies for Europe removed all chance of regaining "even the pre-war [i.e. 1930s!] economic equilibrium". Michel Pablo noted that "the colonial base of the capitalist system is in the process of being broken up". The colonial revolution had "already, for a start, brought European capitalism to its knees". "Thus American imperialism, which is now glutted with productive forces, is obliged to direct its surplus into artificial markets: arms spending, and 'overseas aid'". James P Cannon put it this way: "the world market... no longer offers an adequate outlet for America's glut of capital and surplus goods".

Crises and imperialism: rates of profit and world regimes

The structures of imperialism cannot be deduced from the "shape" of capital in the advanced countries — monopolistic, dominated by finance capital, or whatever. The difference between the modern epoch of finance capital and the earlier one before the First World War is proof enough of that.

More generally, the structure of the world economy cannot be deduced from, or assumed to be parallel to, the structure of national economies. It is, as Trotsky put it, "a mighty and independent reality... which in our epoch imperiously dominates the national markets".

The capitalist world economy has its own laws, its own mutually contradictory tendencies. Competition between nations: the nation-state was the first framework for capitalist development. As capitalism develops, it both outgrows the nation-states and becomes more closely tied up with them. The world economy is therefore an arena not only of competition between capitalists, but also of competition between capitalist states.

Uneven development: capitalist development in a given country creates a spiral of new markets, improved infrastructure, better qualified workers, and attracts new investment there; underdevelopment means small markets, poor infrastructure, under-nourished and ill-trained workers; capitalism therefore has an inbuilt tendency to increase inequality of development between countries.

Expansion: capital has an inbuilt drive to expand, to spread out, and to spread out world-wide.

Combined development: as capitalism expands, it takes the most advanced technology to backward areas. But it also seizes on, uses, and combines itself with, pre-capitalist modes of production where it finds them.

The history of the modern capitalist world economy can be traced through a number of regimes within which those mutually contradictory tendencies have been reconciled for different periods.

There is a general law here of instability of hegemony, too. A dominant position such as that held by Britain in the 19th century or the US since 1945 tends to generate parasitism — high military expenditure; "imperial overstretch"; a slackening of the drive to expand capitalism at home because the capitalists of the dominant nation get comfortable profits from enterprises abroad or from financial operations.

Marx on capitalist crisis

The criterion of the expansion of production is capital itself, the existing level of the conditions of production and the unlimited desire of the capitalists to enrich themselves and to enlarge their capital, but by no means consumption, which from the outset is inhibited...

Moreover, all equalisations are accidental and although the proportion of capital employed in individual spheres is equalised by a continuous process, the continuity of this process itself equally presupposes the constant disproportion which it has continuously, often violently, to even out.

It must never be forgotten, that in capitalist production what matters is not the immediate use-value but the exchange-value and, in particular, the expansion of surplus-value. This is the driving motive of capitalist production, and it is a pretty conception that — in order to reason away the contradictions of capitalist production—abstracts from its very basis and depicts it as a production aiming at the direct satisfaction of the consumption of the producers.

Further: since the circulation process of capital is not completed in one day but extends over a fairly long period until the capital returns to its original form... and great upheavals and changes take place in the market in the course of this period, since great changes take place in the productivity of labour and therefore also in the real value of commodities, it is quite clear, that between the starting-point, the prerequisite capital, and the time of its return at the end of one of these periods, great catastrophes must occur and elements of crisis must have gathered and develop, and these cannot in any way be dismissed by the pitiful proposition that products exchange for products.

The comparison of value in one period with the value of the same commodities in a later period is no scholastic illusion, but rather forms the fundamental principle of the circulation process of capital...

In the crises of the world market, the contradictions and antagonisms of bourgeois production are strikingly revealed. Instead of investigating the nature of the conflicting elements which erupt in the catastrophe, the apologists content themselves with denying the catastrophe itself and insisting, in the face of their regular and periodic recurrence, that if production were carried on according to the textbooks, crises would never occur. Thus the apologetics consist in the falsification of the simplest economic relations, and particularly in clinging to the concept of unity in the face of contradiction.

The real crisis can only be deduced from the real movement of capitalist production, competition and credit.

• From *Theories of Surplus Value, Part 2* by Karl Marx

Keynes : the educated bourgeois

By Martin Thomas

John Maynard Keynes first came to fame in 1919 with a pamphlet that denounced as unworkable the Allies' plan to make defeated Germany pay huge amounts in compensation for World War One. He was active not only as an economic theorist but also as a journalist, civil servant and political figure on the fringes of the Liberal Party.

Through his book, *The General Theory of Employment, Interest and Money* (1936), he fundamentally shifted the terms of orthodox debate on economics.

By the 1920s, orthodox economics had developed a whole theoretical system based on the balancing of supply and demand. At a very high wage, everyone would be keen to work, but the additional production to be got by hiring an extra worker would not be sufficient to make it worthwhile. At a very low wage, demand for labour would be high but many workers would not consider it worth the trouble.

Balance would be reached when the wage was just equal to the additional production got by hiring an extra worker, and just not high enough to persuade the idle and reluctant who remained jobless to offer themselves for work.

For an orthodox economist, therefore, the only possible cause for unemployment (beyond the temporary "between jobs" type) was wages getting stuck at too high a level. As Keynes put it, such an economist "may sympathise with labour in refusing to accept a cut in its money wage ... but scientific integrity forces him to declare that this refusal is, nevertheless, at the root of the trouble".

In fact, most of the economists did not sympathise with labour at all! Their theory was designed to prove that profit was the "natural" reward of capital, and that wages were fixed "naturally" too, so that a fight for better wages could do no good and might even do harm, by causing unemployment.

Their "dismal science" was also designed to prove that governments could do nothing much against unemployment or poverty. When trade unionists demanded better wages or more aid for the jobless, the Treasury would reply: it can't be done! The budget must be balanced! The free market must have its way! Labour governments in 1924 and 1929-31 echoed what the Treasury "experts" told them.

Keynes was no socialist, but he was liberal-minded and instinctively disrespectful of complacent orthodoxy. He argued that unemployment was not caused by high wages, of any other quirk. It was a chronic disease of free-market capitalism.

In the orthodox theory, as Keynes put it, "money makes no real difference except frictionally." It figures only as a convenient token to facilitate exchange , not as a store of value. Keynes looked more closely at the role of money. He showed that, far from automatically balancing supply and demand, the capitalist free market could, and would, produce unsaleable stocks of goods on one side, and needy people unable to buy those goods for lack of cash on another, while piles of idle cash were held by the rich.

Total market demand is made up by consumption and investment. Investment in machinery and equipment, Keynes argued, is determined by the rate of profit which capitalists expect from that investment.

That expected profit rate, he thought, was generally low in mature capitalism. (He explained profits as being due to the "scarcity" of capital: as capital became more plentiful, profits had to decline). At any shock, expectations of profit fall lower still.

Result: a decline in investment. And closely following on that decline will be an increase in the general desire to hold wealth in the form of cash, rather than lending it at interest. The rate of interest will be forced up, worsening the decline of investment by making it harder for entrepreneurs to borrow.

The decline in investment will lead to a much bigger decline in overall effective demand, and therefore in employment, through a process which Keynes called the "multiplier". £1 million less demand for equipment, for example, will mean £1 million less income for workers and capitalists in industry. That in turn will mean less demand for the consumer goods otherwise bought by those people. Suppose they would have spent 80% of the £1 million on consumption, and saved the rest.

Then there is a loss of £800,000 in demand for consumer goods.

That in turn means a further £800,000 loss in incomes; and following on from that, yet another loss in demand, £640,000 this time... When the process has worked itself through, then in this example the total loss of demand is £4 million. And there is a corresponding loss of jobs.

Prices and wages chase each other down a spiral. And, with the rich holding on to their cash, the demand for luxuries and for investment goods remains low, too.

There are counteracting factors; but Keynes saw no reason to suppose that they would be enough to push investment up to a level allowing full employment.

"So, failing some novel expedient, there is no answer to the riddle, except that there must be sufficient unemployment to keep us so poor that our consumption falls short of our income by no more than the equivalent of the physical provision for future consumption which it pays to produce today".

What did Keynes propose? A willingness by central banks to increase the supply of cash in times of downturn, and thus to keep the rate of interest low, would help. That would not, however, be enough. The state must undertake additional investment. If it does so, the multiplier works the other way. £1 million extra spent by the state will produce £4 million total boost to demand, and a corresponding boost to employment.

For the state to "overspend" is not therefore folly: in a slump it is the wisest policy. To balance the government budget is folly.

As the "scarcity-value of capital" falls, the state will gradually have to take a commanding role in investment. "A somewhat comprehensive socialisation of investment will prove the only means of securing an approximation to full employment". This would, however, preserve much of capitalism: it would, indeed, be "the only practicable means of avoiding the destruction of existing economic forms in their entirety" by socialism.

Keynes was something of a snob in his political views. Against Marxism he wrote: "How can I adopt a creed which, preferring the mud to the fish, exalts the boorish proletariat above the bourgeois and the intelligentsia...?" Against the Labour Party his chief complaint was the importance within it of "the trade unionists, once the oppressed, now the tyrants, whose selfish and sectional pretensions need to be bravely opposed".

"Ought I, then, to join the Labour Party: he asked himself. "Superficially that is attractive. But looked at closer. there are great difficulties.

"To begin with, it is a class party, and the class is not my class. I can be influenced by what seems to me to be justice and good sense; but the class war will find me on the side of the educated bourgeoisie".

Yet the main leaders of the labour movement embraced Keynes's theories eagerly. Here was a respected man of science giving support to the view that wage cuts were not the answer to unemployment, and support to their demands for public spending. Here was an alternative to the assaults of the Tories, free from the horrors of revolutionary socialism.

In one sense Keynes was more pessimistic about capitalism than Marx was. Keynes thought capitalism was sinking into a permanent slump, as the rate of profit fell, while Marx argued that capitalism would continue to lurch through booms and slumps as long as the working class did not overthrow it.

Keynes's extreme "pessimism", however, allowed him to conclude that there would be no alternative for the bosses but to accept an increasing role of the state in investment and the "euthanasia of the rentier" — the quiet death of the inactive capitalist who lives off dividends or interest without playing any part in industrial management.

Once the bosses had accepted that, the new state-regulated capitalism would be stable. Thus Keynes transformed his pessimism into optimism.

He complained that "the difficulty is that the capitalist leaders in the City and Parliament are incapable of distinguishing novel measures for safeguarding capitalism from what they call bolshevism", but clearly believed that it was only mental rigidity, not anything more fundamental, which held up the "capitalist leaders" from adopting his "moderately conservative" recommendations.

For Marx, there was no chance that the profiteers would quietly fade away. For Marx, profits are not determined by technology or nature. They are not an index of the "scarcity of capital" (and, in fact, Marx argued, the whole idea of a *long-term* "scarcity" or "excess" of capital is a confusion).

Profits are determined (within limits — but very broad limits) by the class struggle. If profits fall, the profiteers will try to restore them by cutting wages and speeding up labour. They may succeed. If the workers do not overthrow capitalism, then eventually, backed up by the pressure of mass unemployment on the employed workers, the bosses will succeed. They will lay the basis for a new boom.

In that boom, yet again, the accumulation of capital will lurch ahead of the market and the possibilities of profit-making, and the conditions will be created for another slump. The whole process contains vast complexities — many different factors may be the immediate cause of a slump — and the idea of regulating it smoothly by a careful expansion of state investment is fantasy.

For all that, "Keynesian" policies of increased state spending may indeed "work" in the short run to pull the economy out of slumps. The conditions which lead capitalists to subordinate their interests to a "socialisation of investment" by the state are not, however, those of the liberal regime which Keynes hoped for. The most thorough putting into practice of Keynes's recommendations came not through the bright idealists of the New Deal but through the hard-faced men who administered the war economies of 1939-45. When the labour movement embraced Keynes's theories, it tied itself to the chariot of state capitalism, not socialism.

After World War Two, a new bloodless, bowdlerised Keynesianism emerged. The question of falling profits was pushed out of the picture — in the boom of the 1950s and 60s, it looked as if that could be done safely — and the problem was redefined as one of short-term dips in investment below the level needed for full employment, to be corrected by short-term running adjustments to monetary, tax and state spending policies.

Keynesian economists argued that their policy of adjustments to public spending had made capitalism stable. Events were to indicate that the truth was rather the opposite. More than the Keynesian public spending policies permitting capitalist prosperity, it was the capitalist prosperity permitting the public spending policies.

From the early 1970s, capitalism lurched into stagnation and acute instability because of a general decline in its rates of profit and decrease in the viability of its international trading and financial arrangements. Now "Keynesian" public spending brought with them a long list of problems for the capitalist state.

Keynes's had always been a theory which took the national economy as its basic unit, in an epoch when capitalism is

increasingly an integrated international system. Considerations about foreign trade, capital flows, and so on can easily be added to the Keynesian scheme — and, indeed, Keynes himself was an expert on international trade — but the international framework is an extra factor tacked onto the national unit, rather than being the starting point of analysis.

This flaw took its toll in the 1970s. Profits do not come from the natural "scarcity value" of capital: they are an expression of surplus value, the value produced by labour in excess of the amount paid in wages. Public spending is a deduction from that surplus value, it therefore tends to reduce profits. Capitalist states with high public spending tend to lose out in international competition.

Increased public spending and increased employment strengthen workers' fights for higher wages. In a situation where capitalists are desperately striving to reverse a fall in their profit rates, they generally respond by trying to outstrip the higher wages by higher prices. There is an inflationary spiral. Public spending boosts also push up prices directly. Inflation and low interest rates are liable to lead to balance of payments problems.

"Keynesianism" became discredited in the 1970s. It was ousted by new versions of the old pre-Keynesian dogmas. Yet Keynes' criticism of those dogmas has still not been answered.

• From *Workers' Liberty*, June 1996

REBUILDING THE
SOCIALIST MOVEMENT
Fight for a
workers' government!

Two articles, by Martin Thomas

The labour movement can and must push back the Tory government on individual policies. To do more than damage limitation, however, the labour movement needs to drive this government from office.

Seriously to propose policies like heavy taxation of the rich, or expropriation and democratic control of the banks and other big financial outfits, we need also to propose a government which might carry them out.

Yet Labour, under Ed Miliband and Ed Balls, promises only slight tweaks to Osborne's policy. Routine labour movement pressure can make those tweaks bigger, but tweak-plus still falls short of what we need.

These days it falls short of what we need even to stop social regression — widening inequality, increasing subordination of human life to the cruelties of the market, and ecological destruction. Unless we are willing to shrug and accept social regression as inevitable for ourselves and our children, we have to propose something more.

A revolution, one day? Yes, but what now? How can we begin to map out a path from now to a socialist revolution?

Leon Trotsky argued that active socialists should develop "a system of transitional demands, stemming from today's conditions and from today's consciousness of wide layers of the working class, and unalterably leading to one final conclusion: the conquest of power by the proletariat" [working class]. These would be "a bridge between present demands and the socialist program of the revolution".

Progress across the "bridge" depends on how and when large numbers of workers mobilise. That cannot be guaranteed, or predicted exactly, by deft tactics or deft analysis from the active minority. But the transitional-demands approach enables us, as Trotsky put it, to "base our program on the logic of the class struggle".

It cannot enable us to leap ahead from or bypass the working-class struggle; but it can enable us always to be pushing forward.

As a summarising "bridge" demand, knitting together the others and making them coherent, Trotsky proposed "the demand, systematically addressed to the old leadership: 'Break with the bourgeoisie, take the power'...

"Of all parties and organisations which base themselves on the workers... and speak in their name we demand that they break politically from the bourgeoisie and enter upon the road of struggle for the workers' government..." At the same time we agitate for the working-class demands which require a responsive government to carry them out.

In Britain today the "workers' government" means a system of demands aimed at the labour movement:

• Calling for adequate social and economic measures;

• Proposing the radical democratisation of the labour movement, making Labour Party leaders and MPs accountable to the trade unions and local Labour Parties and replacing them where necessary, so that a Labour government can be made to serve the labour movement;

• Advocating a rebuilding and revitalisation of the labour movement at rank and file level, so that left-wing labour-movement policies have real force, rather than being formulas "nodded through".

Workers' Liberty proposes such demands, and works to unite the widest possible working-class ranks round them, including workers who agree on immediate demands but think that our talk of "revolution" is fantasy. In our view, gains on those immediate demands — the creation of a "left Labour" government tied to working-class organisations and interests as closely as the Cameron coalition is to the bankers and bosses — would put the question of "revolution" in a new light.

Q. How would a workers' government come to power? Would it need a revolution, or could a workers' government be elected through the existing parliamentary system?

Genuine working-class revolutions are not explosions dropping from the sky, or military operations concocted by a radical minority. They are the culmination of a vast process of self-awakening, self-education, self-mobilisation by the working class.

Especially in a country with strong parliamentary traditions like Britain, that process can well result in the election of a "left Labour" government before a showdown over state power. In fact, it is unlikely that either the capitalist class or the working class will move the political struggle out of the parliamentary framework without that framework first being tested to the limit. Neither class will decide it has to move outside that framework without first learning by experience.

Once a "left Labour" government is elected, there will then be a battle over whether it becomes a real workers' government — i.e. whether the labour movement is powerful enough to control it and enforce radical measures. If it does, the bourgeoisie will deploy its back-up resources —

the obstructive powers of the House of Lords, the monarchy, and the courts; and, if the elected government defies those unelected powers, then some sort of military coup.

In dull 2012, it seems fantasy to talk about a military coup in Britain. Yet we know, through subsequent admissions by army Chief of Staff Michael Carver, that in February 1974, "fairly senior officers were ill-advised enough to make suggestions that perhaps, if things got terribly bad, the army would have to do something about it".

February 1974 was a time of crisis? But we face, probably, bigger economic crises. No coup actually happened? The Labour government of that time was far from a workers' government. It was a safe administration for the ruling class.

In Australia, as "constitutional" a country as Britain, an only mildly-reforming Labour government was arbitrarily removed from office in November 1975 by the Queen's representative, the Governor-General, using the unelected powers of the monarchy.

In other words, the political struggle would, if the labour movement continued to mobilise, progressively burst out of the parliamentary framework. The labour movement would have to build new organisations like workers' militias and workers' councils. Those new organisations could establish the basis of a victoriously revolutionary workers' government; but they would be formed, in the first place, to defend the reforming parliamentary government.

They would be important instruments by which the labour movement would intervene into the ranks of the armed forces, and, by convincing rank and file soldiers that they should not fire on the working class they came from, help to make the existing unelected state machine unreliable as an instrument of suppression and to break it up and replace it by a new, radically-democratic "semi-state".

The future always turns out richer and more convoluted than we expect. It would be wrong to take a schedule of revolution developing from battles around a left-Labour parliamentary government as a dogma. But an instructive possibility? Yes.

Q. How is "workers' government" different from "socialism"?

In strict Marxist terms, "socialism" is a stage of development a large time after a socialist revolution, achieved only when socialistic development has got far enough to wash away all class conflicts and contrasts.

So a workers' government is different from socialism as the boarding-steps to an airplane are different from the plane's destination. It is also, as we've seen above, a possible phase in the development of a revolution, rather than synonymous with the victorious and consolidated socialist revolution as such.

To counterpose "socialism" as "the answer" to the plight of capitalism is like saying that the answer to the perpetual chill of the Arctic is to move to a warmer climate, without saying how to get there. Not untrue, but not adequate.

Q. How is a "workers' government" different from a reforming Labour government of the 1945 type?

In Britain, a workers' government would probably, in the first place, be a reforming Labour government of a sort — that is, a Labour government based on a revitalised labour movement and mandated by it into radical pro-working-class measures.

But a reforming Labour government may be much less than a workers' government; or (to put it another way) a workers' government of a very limited and stopped-short variety.

The 1945 Labour government introduced reforms, and was much more accountable to the labour movement than recent Labour governments have been. But it built nuclear weapons in secret. It made social cuts (in its later years), kept and used anti-strike legislation, and pursued imperialist wars (Malaya, Korea), all with at best reluctant and forced assent from the labour movement, which remained fairly bureaucratic and passive.

Although the Tories raged in Parliament against measures like the NHS, most ruling-class strategists recognised that in the aftermath of World War they had no choice but to concede reforms, and saw the Labour administration as a relatively "safe" though not ideal vehicle for that.

Q. Does a workers' government require a revolutionary party, or parties, or just a trade-union party?

Not just any labour movement can create a workers' government. Only a mobilised, confident, democratic, and politically-sharp labour movement can do that.

And making the labour movement democratic and politically-sharp is not an automatic process. It requires an agency. It requires the more politically-alert, more revolutionary-minded, more democratically-minded minority to organise in advance, to organise effectively, to develop and redevelop clear ideas and policies, and to win serious influence.

In that sense, a workers' government is impossible without the emergence of at least a minority revolutionary party (though it might conceivably be organised as a tendency within a democratised Labour Party rather than an entirely separate structure). If the inevitable clash between the workers' government and the ruling class is to be resolved in favour of the workers, that revolutionary party will have to grow, in the crisis, to become not just a serious but a decisive influence.

It does not follow that socialists cannot advocate a workers' government without first having a full-scale revolutionary party. It makes no sense to agitate for a workers' government without simultaneously building a revolutionary socialist organisation. But a small revolutionary socialist organisation like Workers' Liberty can use agitation for a workers' government to help educate those around it, to win influence, and to grow.

- From *Solidarity* 244, 2 May 2012

In recent weeks [March 2012[people turning away from ND and Pasok have begun to cluster, not yet around the revolutionary left, but around the reformist left that has opposed the bailout "memorandum" cuts packages.

In the 15 March poll, the Greek Communist Party (KKE), Syriza, and Democratic Left (a splinter from Syriza), totalled 35.5%, about the same as ND and Pasok. Some other recent polls have given them even higher percentages.

To deal with the current crisis, the revolutionary left in Greece has to raise demands like nationalisation under workers' control of the banks and big business, demands which can be implemented only by a government, and not by local struggles, however militant. If the revolutionaries demand the immediate overthrow of the current "technocratic" government, or of a future ND/ Pasok coalition, they need to offer some answers as to what sort of government they want instead.

We should always be cautious about offering tactical demands from a distance. But experience from history suggests three levels at which the questions about government could be given answers of a type that will help take the struggle forward and speed up the crystallisation of a real revolutionary socialist force in the Greek working class.

The first is general advocacy of the type of government which we want to replace the pro-cuts regimes: a workers' government, a government as loyal and as accountable to the working class as the present Greek government is to the bondholders, the bankers, and the capitalists. "Of all parties and organisations which base themselves on the workers", as Leon Trotsky put it, "we demand that they break politically from the bourgeoisie and enter upon the road of struggle for a workers' government... At the same time we indefatigably develop agitation around those transitional demands which should in our opinion form the program of the 'workers' government'."

The second is to look to the organisational recomposition of the Greek labour movement.

The big union federations, GSEE and ADEDY, have as far as I know been very bureaucratic. The union confederation leaderships, financed mainly by allocations from government welfare spending rather than by union dues (which are scarcely collected), stand above a very large number (about 4000) of individual unions, mostly quite small, often limited to single workplaces or cities.

But new connections have been made, notably in the neighbourhood struggles against the new property tax and the threat to cut off electricity to non-payers of that tax. Revolutionaries should argue for the consolidation of those connections into "neighbourhood commissions" like those in Portugal in 1974-5 or in Chile in 1972-3 and for the development of those "commissions" towards real workers' councils. They should explain that those workers' councils could begin to promote workers' control locally and become the base for a workers' government.

Thirdly, revolutionaries should put the reformist left to the test by demanding that they form a united front and agree to collaborate in the creation of an alternative government which would refuse to make the cuts demanded by EU and IMF; nationalise the big banks and businesses under workers' control; and seek to impound the wealth of Greece's ultra-rich.

The approach would be similar to the call which the Bolsheviks made in Russia in 1917 for the reformist left, the Mensheviks and Social Revolutionaries, to break with the "capitalist ministers" in the Provisional Government and form an administration which the Bolsheviks pledged to side with against reaction and to oppose only peacefully.

Paradoxically, the Bolsheviks won over workers and peasants from the Mensheviks and Social Revolutionaries as much by "supporting" them in that sense as by flatly opposing them, and they eventually overthrow the bourgeois Provisional Government on the back not of agitation to bring it down but of "defence" of it against the proto-fascist Kornilov revolt.

Greece is not Russia in 1917. It does not (yet) have workers' councils or dual power. Yet the approach of putting the reformist left to the test could still be valid.

KKE strongly, and maybe unbreakably, opposes a united front. Agitation for a united front could still be a good way for revolutionaries to win over workers attracted to KKE by its pseudo-revolutionary rhetoric.

The Greek revolutionary socialist group Xekinima, linked to the Socialist Party in England, advocates something like this united front agitation, and as far as I can see is right to do so.

• From *Solidarity* 239, 21 March 2012

What is the workers' government?

Excerpts from Leon Trotsky, and from the documents of the Fourth Congress of the Communist International

Report on the 4th Congress (1922), from *The First Five Years of the Comintern, Volume 2*

From the united front flows the slogan of a workers' government. The Fourth Congress submitted it to a thorough discussion and once again confirmed it as the central political slogan for the next period. What does the struggle for a workers' government signify?

We Communists of course know that a genuine workers' government in Europe will be established after the proletariat overthrows the bourgeoisie together with its democratic machinery and installs the proletarian dictatorship under the leadership of the Communist Party. But in order to bring this about it is necessary for the European proletariat in its majority to support the Communist Party.

But this does not obtain as yet and so our Communist parties say on, every appropriate occasion:

"Socialist workers, syndicalist workers, anarchists and non-party workers! Wages are being slashed; less and less remains of the 8-hour working day; the cost of living is soaring. Such things would not be if all the workers despite their differences were able to unite and install their own workers' government."

And the slogan of a workers' government thus becomes a wedge driven by the Communists between the working class and all other classes: and inasmuch as the top circles of the Social Democracy, the reformists, are tied up with the bourgeoisie, this wedge will act more and more to tear away, and it is already beginning to tear away the left wing of Social-Democratic workers from their leaders. Under certain conditions the slogan of a workers' government can become a reality in Europe. That is to say, a moment may arrive when the Communists together with the left elements of the Social Democracy will set up a workers' government in a way similar to ours in Russia when we created a workers' and peasants' government together with the Left Socialist Revolutionaries. Such a phase would constitute a transition to the proletarian dictatorship, the full and completed one. But right now the significance of the slogan of a workers' government lies not so much in the manner and conditions of its realisation in life as in the fact that at the present time this slogan opposes the working class as a whole politically to all other classes, i.e., to all the groupings of the bourgeois political world.

"The slogan of 'The United States of Europe'," June 1923. *The First Five Years of the Comintern, volume 2*

In connection with the slogan of "a workers' and peasants' government", the time is appropriate, in my opinion, for issuing the slogan of "The United States of Europe". Only by coupling these two slogans shall we get a definite systematic and progressive response to the most burning problems of European development...

It might be argued that we are in reality speaking of a European Socialist Federation as an integral part of the future World Federation, and that such a régime can be brought about only by the dictatorship of the proletariat. We shall not, however, pause to answer this argument, since it has been refuted by the international analysis made during the consideration of the question of a "workers' government". "The United States of Europe" is a slogan in every respect corresponding with the slogan "a workers' (or workers' and peasants') government". Is the realization of a "workers' government" possible without the dictatorship of the proletariat? Only a conditional reply can be given to this question. In any case, we regard the "workers' government" as a stage toward the dictatorship of the proletariat. Therein lies the great value of this slogan for us. But the slogan "The United States of Europe" has an exactly similar and parallel significance. Without this supplementary slogan the fundamental problems of Europe must remain suspended in mid-air.

From the ECCI to the Paris Convention of the French Communist Party, September 1922. *The First Five Years of the Comintern, volume 2*

Only a tireless, persistent and flexible propaganda in favour of unity, on the soil of the living facts of mass action, is capable of breaking down the barriers of sectarianism and of shut-in circles within the working class, raising its feeling of class solidarity and thereby necessarily increasing our own influence.

On the basis of all this activity, the slogan of a workers' government, raised at a proper time, could generate a powerful attractive force. At a suitable time, prepared for by events and by our propaganda, we shall address ourselves to the working masses who still reject the revolution and the dictatorship of the proletariat or who have simply not yet matured sufficiently for these questions, and speak to them as follows: "You can now see how the bourgeoisie is restoring its own class unity under the sign of the 'Left Bloc' and is preparing its own 'left' government which actually unifies the bourgeoisie as a whole. Why shouldn't we, the workers, belonging to different parties and tendencies, create together with non-party workers our own proletarian bloc in defence of our own interests? And why shouldn't we put forward our own workers' government?" Here is a natural, simple and clear statement of the whole issue.

But can we Communists conceivably participate in the same government with Renaudel, Blum and the rest?some comrades will ask. Under certain conditions this might prove temporarily unavoidable, just as we Russian Communists were willing, even after our October victory, to permit Mensheviks and SRs to enter the government, and we actually did draw in the Left SRs. But at the present time the question does not, unfortunately, arise in France in such a practical manner. At issue is not the immediate or impending formation of a workers' government with the participation of Frossard and Blum, but rather the question of counterposing agitationally a workers' bloc to the bourgeois bloc. For matters to reach the point of creating a workers' government, it is first necessary to rally the majority of the working class around this slogan. Once we achieve this, that is, the moment when the worker-Dissidents and the members of the General Confederation of Labour demand a united labour government, the stock of Renaudel, Blum and Jouhaux would not be worth much, because these gentlemen are able to maintain themselves only through an alliance with the bourgeoisie, provided the working class is split.

It is perfectly obvious that once the majority of the French working class unites under the banner of a workers' government, we shall have no cause whatever to worry about the composition of this government. A genuine success for the slogan of a workers' government would already signify, in the nature of things, the prelude to the proletarian revolution. This is what those comrades fail to understand who approach slogans formally and assay them with the yardstick of verbal radicalism, without taking into account the processes occurring within the working class itself.

Fourth Congress of the Communist International (1922), Theses on Tactics

The slogan of a workers' government (or a workers' and peasants' government) can be used practically everywhere as a general agitational slogan. However, as a central political slogan, the workers' government is most important in countries where the position of bourgeois society is particularly unstable and where the balance of forces between the workers' parties and the bourgeoisie places the question of government on the order of the day as a practical problem requiring immediate solution. In these countries the workers' government slogan follows inevitably from the entire united front tactic.

62

The parties of the Second International are trying to rescue the situation in these countries by advocating and forming a coalition of the bourgeoisie and the social democrats. The recent attempts by certain parties of the Second International (e.g. in Germany) to take part in this kind of coalition government secretly, whilst refusing to be openly involved, are nothing but a manoeuvre to pacify the indignant masses, just a more subtle deception of the working masses. In place of a bourgeois/social-democratic coalition, whether open or disguised, Communists propose a united front involving all workers, and a coalition of all workers' parties around economic and political issues, which will fight and finally overthrow bourgeois power. Following a united struggle of all workers against the bourgeoisie, the entire state apparatus must pass into the hands of a workers' government, so strengthening the position of power held by the working class.

The most elementary tasks of a workers' government must be to arm the proletariat, disarm the bourgeois counter-revolutionary organisations, bringing control over production, shift the main burden of taxation onto the propertied classes and break the resistance of the counter-revolutionary bourgeoisie.

Such a workers' government is possible only if it is born out of the struggle of the masses and is supported by combative workers' organisations formed by the most oppressed sections of workers at grassroots level. However, even a workers' government that comes about through an alignment of parliamentary forces, i.e., a government of purely parliamentary origin, can give rise to an upsurge of the revolutionary workers' movement. It is obvious that the formation of a genuine workers' government, and the continued existence of any such government committed to revolutionary politics, must lead to a bitter struggle with the bourgeoisie or even to civil war. The mere attempt by the proletariat to form such a workers' government will from its very first days come up against extremely strong resistance from the bourgeoisie. The slogan of a workers' government therefore has the potential to rally the proletarians and unleash revolutionary struggle.

In certain circumstances, Communists must declare themselves ready to form a workers' government with non-Communist workers' parties and workers' organisations. However, they should do so only if there are guarantees that the workers' government will conduct a real struggle against the bourgeoisie of the kind already outlined. The obvious conditions on which Communists will participate in such a government are:

1 Communists participating in such a government remain under the strictest control of their Party;

2. Communists participating in such a workers' government should be in extremely close contact with the revolutionary organisations of the masses;

3. The Communist Party has the unconditional right to maintain its own identity and complete independence of agitation.

For all its great advantages, the slogan of a workers' government also has its dangers, as does the whole tactic of the united front. To avoid these dangers and to confront now the illusion that the stage of 'democratic coalition' is inevitable, the Communist Parties must be aware of the following:

Every bourgeois government is simultaneously a capitalist government, but not every workers' government is a truly proletarian, socialist government.

The Communist International must consider the following possibilities:

1. A liberal workers' government, such as existed in Australia and is possible in Britain in the near future.

2. A social-democratic 'workers' government' (Germany).

3. A workers' and peasants' government. Such a possibility exists in the Balkans, Czechoslovakia, etc.

4. A social-democratic/Communist coalition government.

5. A genuine proletarian workers' government, which can be created in its pure form only by a Communist Party.

Communists are also prepared to work alongside those workers who have not yet recognised the necessity of the dictatorship of the proletariat. Accordingly Communists are also ready, in certain conditions and with certain guarantees, to support a non-Communist workers' government. However, the Communists will still openly declare to the masses that the workers' government can be neither won nor maintained without a revolutionary struggle against the bourgeoisie.

The first two types of workers' governments (the workers' and peasants' and the social-democratic/Communist governments) fall short of representing the dictatorship of the proletariat, but are still an important starting-point for the winning of this dictatorship. The complete dictatorship of the proletariat can only be a genuine workers' government (type 5) consisting of Communists.

Anti-capitalist, pro-what?

By Rhodri Evans

On 28 April seventy or eighty activists came together in London, at a meeting primarily organised by a group of people (Simon Hardy, Luke Cooper, and others) who had just quit the Workers' Power organisation. The meeting set up an "Anti-Capitalist Initiative".

The initiative will start a website for coordination and discussion; establish a coordinating group; and have a day or weekend school in the summer, a conference in the autumn.

It wants "unity and co-operation"; to "overcome division and sectarianism"; and "wider discussion".

This open letter, addressed both to the ex-WP grouping and to the wider range of activists in the new "Initiative", offers some ideas about how those aims can be advanced and about pitfalls on the way.

United front and party

Every battle in the working-class struggle, or for liberation, requires broad unity. A strike has to unite workers in a workplace or sector irrespective of their views on the Middle East, China, religion, or even, say, cuts in general.

Anti-cuts, anti-fascist, and similar campaigns require unity, too.

If our aim is not just to fight immediate battles, but to replace capitalism altogether by a free cooperative commonwealth, then, as well as the broadly-uniting campaigns, we also need a political organisation developing and advocating that wider aim.

Marxists argue that the social revolution finds its agency in the working class, and its force in the organisation and self-education that the working class develops through daily struggles. If that is so, then, to be effective, the organisation advocating the social revolution must develop and organise for coherent views not just on the future and general revolutionary aim, but on the strategy and tactics of working-class and other liberation struggles now. It must be an active party and not just a group making propaganda for a future ideal.

In other words, we need two different types of organisation simultaneously, On the one hand, unions and other united-front organisations, which have to be broad if they are to be effective, and which have more limited remits, shorter-term outlooks, and are looser. And, on the other, political party or proto-party organisations, which are smaller, but which, if lucid, may do valuable educational and catalytic work even when small.

Revolutionary-socialist parties or proto-parties, because of their more complex and long-term tasks, are inherently more likely to splinter than united-front campaigns. And those united-front campaigns need to draw in people with different, or no definite, views on longer-term perspectives.

The different revolutionary-socialist parties or proto-parties need to be able to cooperate with each other, and with reformist or agnostic-minded people, in unions and campaigns.

In the new network, we will be proposing that it cooperate with others to:

• Set up a united coordination for campaigns for the NHS;

• Build the new rank-and-file initiative among school workers (conference on 16 June) and, where possible, similar initiatives in other trade-union sectors;

• Revive and continue united anti-cuts committees based on local labour movements;

• Develop the National Campaign Against Fees and Cuts among students.

The network would do best to work with others in broad united fronts on immediate active campaigns, rather than constituting itself as yet another "rival" campaign group on cuts, the NHS, or whatever.

We will also be proposing that the network set aside time for self-education and structured debate on longer-term strategic questions, some of which we will indicate below in discussing the ex-WP grouping's statement.

Some participants in the new network think it is a broad coalition, operating largely by consensus, maybe providing a forum for different left currents and unaffiliated activists to liaise and debate in a way they now usually fail to. The ex-WP group's statement suggest they see it more as a "stepping stone" to a party-type group which is (as they put it) "clear on strategic questions".

This ambiguity could be harmful. There is a risk of botching it so as to function well neither as united-front campaign, nor as broad forum, nor as party-type organisation.

What organisation for what unity

The ex-WP statement is centred round the aim of establishing "a new plural and broader anti-capitalist organisation", "a new group" (though "not overnight").

One paragraph states the aim as "a united, plural organisation in which splits can be avoided and the inevitable differences are factored into the day to day practice... debate [but] practical unity where we agree".

If the practical unity is only "where we agree", then the model here is a loose coordination of different groupings, or a consensus-decision-making collective. It's an organisation looser than, for example, a trade union, which often obliges all members to join a practical action even though not all agree. (Few strike votes have a 100% majority).

Another paragraph gives a different line: the new organisation would have "democratic centralism [but meaning] unity in action around democratically determined goals, and free and open discussion".

This suggests something less loose than a union, and maybe more like a party, though maybe (it's not clear) a deliberately loose party which would not strive for clarity on longer-term perspectives but instead agree to differ on such things and confine itself (as unions generally do) to taking decisions where a majority binds a minority only on selected immediate activities.

Another passage offers a third variant, when it calls for "uniting sections of the left around a strategic perspective... clear on the strategic questions", which implies a less loose "party", with a defined and obligatory "line" on strategic as well as immediate issues.

All those variants look like different versions of a regroupment of fragments and individuals broadly on the political wavelength of WP — a new grouping, wider than WP and to one degree or another looser, smaller and slower-paced than the more active revolutionary-socialist groups, SWP, SP, or Workers' Liberty.

Other paragraphs suggest that the new initiative will bypass and eclipse the whole existing activist left, and catapult itself straight into the status of an electoral mass party, "into the mainstream" of politics, into becoming able to "present a credible alternative to the mainstream parties".

"Galloway's success shows what is possible, as does the support for Mélenchon in France".

Recent polls show long-term mass disaffection with the long-established major parties.

But neither Galloway nor Mélenchon is anti-capitalist in the sense of fighting for the expropriation of the capitalist class and the replacement of market-based economy by a free cooperative commonwealth.

Galloway has said: "my main political mistake, in retrospect, was that state ownership of the means of production, distribution and exchange, in which I believed, and for which I campaigned, was a false God... I'm not saying, at all, that everything in the private garden is rosy. There's just more flowers than there were in the state garden".

Mélenchon's Front de Gauche programme ("L'humain d'abord") proposes "a public pole" in finance, "public poles" in industry, and, in the longer term, "new powers for workers in the running of their workplaces". It's something like a 1970s Labour Party programme.

Mélenchon's vote represents a constituency of great importance for revolutionary socialists in France, but it would be foolish to read it as showing the rise of a fresh new left. The left-of-SP vote in France in 2012 was smaller than in 2002 or 1995. The main activist force behind Mélenchon is the far-from-fresh-and-new French Communist Party.

Galloway cannot be equated with Mélenchon, who is an honest left social-democrat. Bradford West shows, sadly, that it possible for the current disaffection to be channelled by a demagogue with a horrible record. It is possible for the disaffection to be channelled by the far right, too.

A revolutionary socialist party which had built a sufficient activist base and profile might well be able to use the mass disaffection reflected in the polls to make rapid advances through electoral activity. But not even Mélenchon shows us an example of how to leapfrog the difficulties of getting that activist base and profile in the first place.

We could pretend to leapfrog by attaching ourselves to the coat-tails of Mélenchon, or Galloway, claiming their electoral scores as somehow ours, and imagining that we are catapulted by proxy "into the mainstream". But it would be self-deception. The SWP found that with Galloway in Respect.

In any case, what has the Galloway-Mélenchon tack got to do with the project of an *"anti-capitalist* initiative"? Nothing much, unless the term "anti-capitalist" be used so broadly as to cover all dissatisfaction with the obviously "capitalist" features of present-day society and desire to alleviate them in some way or another.

The negative term "anti-capitalist" (pro-what?) has drawbacks anyway. In the broadest usage it would notionally embrace a coalition stretching through the soft left to populist Tories and far-rightists.

The ex-WP grouping writes that for them the "anti-capitalist initiative" is "not an end in itself" but a "stepping stone for something greater". Other activists in the initiative should ask the ex-WP grouping to think through, and spell out, more about whose boots will be "stepping" on them, and in which direction.

Why quit Workers' Power

On the whole, the "stepping stone" seems to be intended to step towards a regroupment of fragments on the broad WP wavelength, "different, more plural, more open, much looser", but "still clear" (by WP reckoning) "on the strategic questions". The Galloway-Mélenchon allusion gives colouring, but has little practical bite.

Whether things will work out in the direction of a broad WP-ish regroupment is another matter. Many, perhaps most, of the participants in local "anti-capitalist" groups — which are scheduled, on current plans, to be autonomous — may prefer otherwise. They may prefer to maintain local clearing-houses for activities and left discussions, of a type that has long existed on and off, in smaller cities especially, rather than be made "stepping stones" towards "clarity" (WP-style) "on the strategic questions".

The ex-WP group's statement says that for them "a parting of the ways" [from WP] "became necessary" because of the WP majority's "conservative intransigence... to alter course on fundamentals".

Oddly, however, their statement expresses no wish for WP to "alter course on fundamentals"... or on any detail of political position.

They say that WP is right on fundamentals. It was from WP, they say, that they "learnt the foundation of their Marxist ideas". They seem just as reluctant as the WP majority to "alter course" on those "fundamentals".

The statement objects (rightly, we think) to WP's rule obliging its members to pretend public unanimity — "revolutionary organisations should conduct their debates in private and only present their conclusions to the class". But now the ex-WP people are released from that rule, and can express their differences of opinion publicly, they apparently have none to express.

Why then the talk of "critique", "re-evaluation", and "blue skies discussion"? The writers paradoxically combine assent to *WP's version of* Marxism with not-spelled-out doubt about the Leninist-Trotskyist tradition generally and even (as we shall see) about Marxism generally.

They write that they reject "a method of organising exclusively focused on building specifically Leninist-Trotskyist groups". That clause makes sense only if the term "exclusively" is taken as idle polemical flourish and deleted.

Neither WP nor anyone else advocates "organising *exclusively* focused on building specifically Leninist-Trotskyist groups", nor could they, because it is basic to a Leninist-Trotskyist approach that we also work to build trade unions, campaigns, united fronts, etc. And the rest of the ex-WP statement indicates that they wish to build "a new group", though not "overnight", which will be "much looser" not only than WP's mode *but also than "specifically Leninist-Trotskyist" operation.*

The ex-WP group claimed that they "showed in the course of the debate that [a more relaxed approach] was the norm in the revolutionary movement in the decades prior to 1917".

That clause suggests a desire to go back to the Second International's model of slow-moving, consensus-seeking "all-inclusive parties" — which, to be sure, was more civilised and intellectually richer than the WP-type regime today.

The Bolsheviks at the time thought of themselves as simply applying in the different conditions of Russia the methods advocated by Karl Kautsky and others in the West. In fact they developed a different method, geared to building a party that was politically sharp and quick on its feet. But they did not crystallise and codify that difference until after 1917.

Implicitly the ex-WP group accept the WP majority's mode as the authentic continuation of the post-1917 "Leninist-Trotskyist" approach. They take the fact of similar regimes to WP's in SWP, SP, and so on, as proof that the left's current poor state is due to us being "focused on building specifically Leninist-Trotskyist groups".

But the problem with the left is not being "too Trotskyist". The SLL in the 60s built an organisation of some clout, far more at least than the new anti-capitalist initiative can hope to acquire short of a miracle. The IS/SWP did likewise in the 70s, and Militant in the 80s.

Those groups collapsed, shrivelled, or fell back not because they were too Trotskyist, but because they were not Trotskyist enough. They inclined to short-sighted opportunism.

We cannot build a large new revolutionary socialist organisation just by a snap of the fingers; but we will serve the young activists of the next big wave of working-class radicalisation very badly if we use these years of preparation to drill ourselves and those around us in the idea of being "looser", less "Leninist-Trotskyist".

We urge the ex-WP group to undertake a broader discussion, with Workers' Liberty and with others, on this question.

Here as on many other questions, WP's mode is not an authentic continuation of the "Leninist-Trotskyist" approach, but a kitsch compilation of strands and shreds from the tradition of Lenin and Trotsky. It is heavily skewed by the cultural pressure on that tradition, for decades, of Stalinism (and by some of the exaggerations and one-sidednesses which were introduced into Bolshevik discourse under pressure of civil war in Russia).

A "model of democratic centralism that states revolutionary organisations should conduct their debates in private and only present their conclusions to the class" (as ex-WP put it) is not the only alternative to a loose "all-inclusive" alliance; it is not authentically Bolshevik or Trotskyist; and in any case it cannot serve revolutionary socialists who want to continue and build on what the Bolsheviks taught us about the need for a party which is politically sharp and quick on its feet, as distinct from the model of pre-World-War-One social democracy.

Workers' Liberty's constitution states that Workers' Liberty members are obliged *not* to pretend to hold views which they don't really agree with. If they are in a minority, they should state what the majority view is, as fairly as they can; they should unite with the majority in action (votes, participation in campaigns or whatever); they should not express their dissent in such a way as to undermine majority-decided action; but they should not pretend that their own views are any other than what they really are.

They are also *obliged* to express their dissenting views internally. We are obliged always to strive to convince each other and reach the clearest conclusion, rather than to "agree to disagree".

As anyone can see from scanning the files of our publications or the archives of our website, our custom and practice is that minorities have space in our press to present their views publicly (though the majority retains the right to decide how and when: if the AWL majority decision is to

70

continue with a strike but a minority favours a return to work, the minority does not have the right to an article in our paper agitating for a return to work). It is also usual that minorities are given time to speak at our summer schools, public meetings, and so on.

This approach makes our organisation less brittle. Minorities inside Workers' Liberty are still dissatisfied, of course; but they do not have the additional split-provoking aggravation of being compelled publicly to spout views which they really reject.

And, we believe, it also makes us more effective. If we "only present our conclusions to the class", stripped of the debates that make sense of the conclusions, then we cannot hope to convince workers.

If we are compelled to go through the motions of arguing views which we do not agree with, then that can only corrupt and spoil, in us, the revolutionary ardour for truth which is the basic asset in all effective Marxist agitation.

Only by training ourselves always to use our brains and voices to enlighten rather than to obscure, always to seek for and spread the truth rather than "what will go down well" or what "won't get us into trouble", can we make ourselves effective revolutionary socialists.

Dialogue between left groups

As well as setting rules for procedure among ourselves, Workers' Liberty also fights for a regime of honest dialogue among groups on the left.

Workers' Liberty, like all other groups, learns not only from our internal debates, but from the debate and dialogue we have with those around us. Our rules about our members not pretending to have views other than their real ones are designed also to make us more able to get into real dialogue with people around us; to listen to people around us who may have more knowledge, or different insights, on some issues than anyone in Workers' Liberty; and thus to learn.

As can be seen from the record of our summer schools and public meetings, we consistently seek debate with other groups on the left.

In so doing, we combat a culture on the left today where most groups wall off their members by caricature misrepresentation of other tendencies.

For all their talk of "critical re-evaluation", "plurality", "debate as a good thing", and so on, the ex-WP people are still caught in that culture.

In a letter to WP, they declare indignantly that "we have never advocated, for example, a unity drive towards the Alliance for Workers' Liberty as part of the new project in Britain, because we recognise that they are a pro-imperialist sect that are very much outside of what we consider to be the proper parameters of a common revolutionary organisation..."

When they left WP and Workers' Liberty asked to meet them to talk about possibilities for practical collaboration and for debate and discussion, the ex-WP group immediately said that it was "unlikely" that they would agree to any such meeting.

Evidently the ex-WP group fear being denounced by the WP majority as "soft on the AWL". In order to fend off such denunciation, they resort to slander.

In no conflict or question has AWL taken a "pro-imperialist" position. WP's critical support in the 1980s for the Russian occupation in Afghanistan was pro-imperialist if you consider the USSR imperialist, or not if you don't. Assent to Saddam Hussein's seizure of Kuwait in 1990 was "pro-imperialist" if you consider Saddam's Iraq to have been a regional imperialist now, not if you don't. But there is no issue on which the AWL's position has been "pro-imperialist", however wide the range of states you consider "imperialist".

An argument could be made that "Third Camp" positions which we have taken led to insufficient agitational vigour in combatting the policies of the US and its allies in some issues. We would reply that honest, lucid explanation of the issues — including when the US and its allies face opponents which are themselves utterly reactionary or regional-imperialist — is more important. There is a real debate to be had there.

We should have the debate, and not have it pushed aside by a bland statement that Workers' Liberty is "pro-imperialist" and "outside the proper parameters".

The political platform

The ex-WP statement includes a paragraph which appears intended to summarise where they stand politically.

"We are committed to taking steps towards an anti-capitalist organisation that is opposed to austerity, privatisation, racism, sexism, imperialist war and supports the Palestinians. We believe that mass strikes and demonstrations are needed to bring down the government. We support the building of a rank and file movement across the unions, an essential goal in the context of the pensions sell out by sections of the union movement. We are committed to working towards unity in the anticuts movement and overcoming unnecessary divisions which hinder our movement. We still believe that the working class is a crucial agent of revolutionary change, though we want to explore new and more creative ways of fusing socialist ideas with the kind of struggles that are going on today".

It is an odd mixture of generalities and immediate tactical positions.

We agree about about the building of a rank and file movement. (That idea is one of the recognisable elements that WP retains from its past when, as the Left Platform in IS/SWP, it was largely formed politically by the influence of our tendency). We agree, of course, about unity in the anti-cuts movement.

Almost anyone describing themselves as "on the left" would agree about opposing "austerity, privatisation, racism, sexism, and imperialist war".

The other elements in the brief statement of political position call for some analysis.

a. "Supports the Palestinians"

In the ex-WP's statement-of-position paragraph, the first sentence states the basic parameters; the next three more detailed, immediate, and tactical positions; and the last one a theoretical overview.

That first sentence is odd. It provides five stances of opposition — to capitalism, austerity, privatisation, racism, sexism, imperialist war — and only one assertion of what the group is *for*.

The one thing they say are *for* is not a social principle or project, but... a nationality! They support... one of the several hundred nationalities into which bourgeois society has divided humanity.

Maybe "support the Palestinians" is shorthand for "support the national rights of the Palestinians", and the Palestinians are specially mentioned because they are an oppressed nation? Why then the Palestinians but not the Kurds, Tibetans, Chechens, Tamils, Sahrawi and so on?

For WP, "support the Palestinians" means wanting "to 'abolish' in the course of the struggle" Israel and to subsume the Israel-Jewish nation into a single state covering all pre-1948 Palestine, with a presumed Arab majority and hegemony.

Workers' Liberty says Israel should get out of the West Bank and clear the way for the Palestinians' right, and majority demand, for a fully independent state alongside Israel.

That democratic programme, recognising the right to national self-determination of both Palestinian Arabs and Israeli Jews, is the only way to win Arab-Jewish workers' unity and start building a movement which can create a socialist united states of the Middle East.

We read the phrase "support the Palestinians" in the ex-WP statement as code for "have the WP position on Israel-Palestine". We suspect this specific policy is included in such a short summary paragraph for the same reason that the sentence about "broad unity, but not with the AWL" in their letter to WP.

Better to state things openly, and debate them openly.

b. "Strikes to bring down the government"

The statement's sentence — "we believe that mass strikes and demonstrations are needed to bring down the government" — is nonsense. The government is more likely to be brought down by a routine general election, or by an ordinary parliamentary scandal which disrupts the Tory/ Lib-Dem alliance.

Is the intended meaning that "mass strikes and demonstrations" would be the *best* way to bring down the government?

A false implication is hidden here, and a question is begged.

The false implication is we should desire "mass strikes and demonstrations" *because* they are the best way to bring down the government. That is not true.

We desire intelligently-conducted, well-organised "mass strikes and demonstrations" (the qualification is important) because they enable workers to win gains and improve their self-confidence, political awareness, and organisation.

If mass strikes reach such a level that they may bring down the government, then it is vital that they have solid and well-understood *other* goals than just bringing down the government, goals which they will insist on and continue action for even after the government falls, if it does.

Mass strikes on a scale which makes the government unable to continue constitute a semi-revolutionary crisis. But if leftists have told workers that bringing down the government is the supreme prize *even for mass strikes on a semi-revolutionary scale*, then they make it easier for the ruling class to evade the crisis by calling elections.

The ruling class can then escape with nothing worse than having to transfer governmental office to the "loyal opposition", such as exists in Britain in the shape of the Labour Party and in all long-established bourgeois regimes in some shape or another. And it may not even have to do that: the experience of France in 1968 and Australia in 1975 suggests that a mass strike wave against a hated government which lets itself be quelled by the calling of elections is likely to lead to a conservative victory in the polls, thanks to the votes of millions of people scared by the strikes but seeing the working class as unable to win any positive social transformation.

For now — i.e. short of semi-revolutionary mass strikes — to install a Labour government in place of the current coalition, and sooner rather than later, would be a step forward. Since the unions still have decisive voting power within Labour, it would open the possibility of enforcing concessions, or advancing working-class political organisation and awareness by sharpening contradictions within the labour movement, or both.

But that "bringing down the government" — i.e. replacing it by Labour — is in fact a step forward depends on an assessment of the Labour Party. Under Blair and Brown, it would have been a step forward if Blair or Brown had been ejected from leadership by the labour movement. It would *not* have been a step forward if social unrest had led to the collapse of the government and its replacement, inevitably, by the Tories or a Tory-led coalition.

The phrase in the statement begs the question of a serious discussion about the Labour Party.

Working-class

"Working class a crucial agent, though..."

The paragraph's final sentence states a theoretical perspective. "We still believe that the working class is *a* crucial agent of revolutionary change, though *we want to explore new and more creative ways of fusing socialist ideas with the kind of struggles that are going on today*" (emphasis added).

The replacement of the Marxist idea that the working class is *the* gravedigger of capitalism by the vaguer term, "a crucial agent", cannot be a writer's accident here, since it is given emphasis by the qualifications "still" and "though..."

The proposition that the working class is *a* crucial agent of revolutionary change has nothing specifically Marxist about it at all, and would hardly be questioned even by, say, anarchists of Murray Bookchin's stripe, who explicitly reject the Marxist idea of the working class as the only really revolutionary class.

What are the ex-WP group's considered thoughts on this issue? It should be openly discussed.

The qualifying clause is odd: "though we want to explore new and more creative ways of fusing socialist ideas with the kind of struggles that are going on today".

New and more creative ways of promoting socialist ideas are always desirable. How can the idea of better agitation, explanation, and dialogue be a qualification — a "though..." clause — to the proposition that the working class is a crucial agent of change? It makes no sense.

The underlying thought may be decoded by studying the word "fusing", odd in this context. What does it mean to "fuse" socialist ideas with struggles? If the writer means using socialist ideas to guide intervention in those struggles, or winning participants in those struggles over to socialist views, why not say so, rather than using the word "fuse", which does not fit?

Even half-literally, "fusing" socialist ideas with, say, an anti-fascist campaign would mean that campaign becoming completely identified with socialist ideas and socialist ideas becoming completely identified with that campaign. But we do not want that! We want anti-fascist campaigns to mobilise many workers who are not yet socialists, and socialist ideas must be, and be seen as, of much wider scope than anti-fascist campaigning.

Probably the writer has picked up the word "fusing", consciously or unconsciously, from its best-known use in the revolutionary socialist tradition, in Lenin's writings in the Iskra period, 1900-03.

Lenin in turn took it from Karl Kautsky's 1892 commentary on the Erfurt Programme, a text which was the main handbook for socialists across the world in its time.

For Kautsky the term fusion (or merger, or amalgamation, which can also be and often have been English translations of Kautsky's German word) was exactly appropriate. He was talking about the coming-together into a single movement of two previously separate ones, the socialist movement and the organic workers' movement.

In his commentary Kautsky said that the socialist movement first emerged separate from and even partly antagonistic to the organised workers' movement, i.e. primarily the trade unions and worker-dominated movements for democratic rights. The socialists, groups of Blanquist conspirators or Fourierist or Owenite or Saint-Simonian or Cabetist or Proudhonist colony-builders or scheme-sketchers, saw no relevance in trade-union wage battles.

There was a "chasm between socialism and the militant proletariat". "If the socialist movement and the labour movement were ever to become one it was necessary for socialism to be raised beyond the utopian point of view. To accomplish this was the illustrious work of Marx and Engels".

Marx and Engels developed a theory which showed socialism as an organic development of the logic of class struggle within capitalism. That opened the way for more worker-activists to become convinced that socialism was the logical summary and goal of all their detailed immediate efforts, and for socialists to root their efforts in workers' struggles.

"A great change came with the amalgamation of the socialist movement and the labour movement. Now the proletariat has a goal toward which it is struggling, which it comes nearer to with every battle. Now all features of the class-struggle have a meaning, even those that produce no immediately practical results".

Kautsky did not take account of how the fused socialist-and-labour movement would later be bureaucratised and conservatised, but for his argument in 1892, as far as it went, his term fusion makes sense. It *only* makes sense on the basis of the Marxist theory of socialism as the logic of specifically *working-class* struggle.

The "though..." clause in the ex-WP statement can only signify that the writer thinks that "the kind of struggles that are going on today" are not working-class struggles of the sort Kautsky had in mind, but more diffuse "social-movement" things. Despairing of finding working-class struggles with which to "fuse" the socialist movement, the writer expresses a vague hope that the socialist movement can instead be nourished by non-worker struggles (although with, still, "a crucial" contribution from the working class).

Revolutionary socialists absolutely should support, intervene in, and seek to win activists in non-worker struggles for liberation. Lenin insisted on that idea in exactly the same writings of 1900-03 in which he constantly referred to Kautsky's "fusion" formula.

But "socialist ideas" can be "fused" with all those diverse struggles only if those socialist ideas are diluted into a vague and generic opposition to oppression.

Kitsch Trotskyism

In our view, elements of the ex-WP group's statement of political position derive from insufficiently-rethought recycling of what they were taught as "Marxist ideas" in WP.

And yet the statement contains a passage which points to some of what is wrong with WP's version of "Marxism". "The way that Marxism came to be conceived as a result led to a narrowness; thinkers outside of the Marx-Engels-Lenin-Trotsky (and partially Luxemburg) axis tended to be subjected to a form of black and white critique that undermined the kind of engagement necessary for a living and evolving body of thought to develop. This naturally places constraints on critical thinking as the concern to 'get it right' tends to undermine the development of an attitude that recognises that a degree of plurality in the evolution of ideas is necessary to try and uncover objective truth..."

The initial Workers' Power group split away from our tendency in 1976 on the basis not of any large political differences but of a claim that they were creative thinkers with special expertise in dynamic, agitational, industrial mass work, and we were crabby sectarians and propagandists.

That soon rang hollow. So the WP core which "sweated it out" had to construct other points of difference. They did it by cut-and-pasting, one after another, excerpts of so-called "orthodox Trotskyism".

As Clement Greenberg wrote: "The precondition for kitsch... is the availability close at hand of a fully matured cultural tradition, whose discoveries, acquisitions, and perfected self-consciousness kitsch can take advantage of for its own ends. It borrows from it devices, tricks, stratagems, rules of thumb, themes... It draws its life blood, so to speak, from this reservoir of accumulated experience". It offers up "the miraculous and the sympathetic" in synthetic, easily-satisfying form.

WP became the most kitsch of all kitsch-Trotskyist groups. For it, a narrowly-defined doctrinal tradition became a source of quotabilities to rationalise positions. All theorising outside that canon became items to be ticked or crossed — "black and white" — in somewhat the same style as the name index in old Moscow editions of Marx and Engels would list thinkers, each checked as "idealist" or "materialist".

Workers' Liberty works to be *more* "doctrinaire" than the other tendencies, in that we work to educate our members in the Marxist classics and constantly to check our ideas against the classics. We also work to be — and are — the *least* doctrinaire, in that we are frequently willing to say that a classic "text" is inapplicable to a current problem, or another classic "text" is wrong.

In the 1930s Trotsky analysed the Soviet Union as a "degenerated workers' state". By the end of World War Two, with the USSR overrunning Eastern Europe and the emergence of new Stalinist states, it was clear that the argument had to be reassessed, and in fact Trotsky had been wrong.

"Orthodox" Trotskyists ossified Trotsky's position into a rigid and nonsensical dogma, in which the Stalinist states remained workers' states, whatever the position of the workers, as long as the means of production were nationalised.

The original Workers Power group had drifted away from Cliff's version of state capitalism without settling on an alternative. As it sought to solidify itself after the 1976 split, under vigorous pressure from the then-bustling Spartacist group, it needed an orthodoxy.

It eventually announced that events had convinced it the USSR was a workers' state — and when? Of all times, in 1979/80, after Russian invaded Afghanistan! On that basis it refused to call for Russian troops to withdraw.

Today WP and all its splits continue to maintain that *North Korea* is a "bureaucratically deformed workers' state", the only place outside Cuba where the working class still somehow rules.

That view skews the WP/ex-WP overview of the whole history of the last century. It skews their picture of where we, they, and the working class are in history. It must have helped nourish the thought that socialist ideas can be "fused" with diverse non-worker struggles just as well as with working-class battle.

And it also sets a template for the WP/ex-WP view on forces like the Taliban, the Sunni-supremacist Iraqi "resistance" of 2004-8, Saddam Hussein, etc.: by virtue of the negative fact of coming into conflict with the dominant advanced-capitalist power, the USA, they fill the role (left vacant by the collapse of most of the Stalinist states) of big forces, 'objectively' on our side, though not as we would wish.

In 2004, at the European Social Forum in London, WP took part in an attempt to 'no platform' an Iraqi trade unionist because of the Stalinist/reformist Iraqi Communist Party's collaboration with the American occupation authorities. They insisted that this representative of Iraq's really existing workers' movement, re-emerging after more than thirty years of repression, be not allowed to speak. At the same time they supported the "resistance" militias which as well as fighting the occupation were conducting sectarian terror and harassing and murdering union activists.

The ex-WP group is right to call for "critical re-evaluation" and "open, 'blue-skies' discussion". But if it comes to mean a project of pulling together a loose regroupment, politically broadly WP but tacitly less "Leninist-Trotskyist", tacitly less insistent on the centrality of working-class struggles, that will be wrong.

• WP split statement: http://links.org.au/node/2825
• WP response: http://www.fifthinternational.org/content/statement-resignations-british-section-league
• Decisions from 28 April: www.permanentrevolution.net/entry/3400
• Anti-capitalist initiative website: http://www.anticapitalists.org

What is the Bolshevik-Trotskyist tradition?

By Sean Matgamna

Introduction

What follows is a summary of the political and ideological traditions on which *Workers' Liberty* and *Solidarity* base ourselves.

Isaac Newton famously summed up the importance of studying, learning, and building on forerunners. "If I have seen a little further it is by standing on the shoulders of giants", he wrote, referring to René Descartes, his contemporary Robert Hooke, and presumably also to his direct predecessor Isaac Barrow.

In science few people think they can neglect the "tradition" and rely on improvisation. In politics, alas, too many.

The summary here, written in 1995, starts as follows: "Living in an age of apostasy to socialism and Marxism, and of a great turning of backs on the past, it is necessary for us to publicly identify and proclaim our roots and traditions". That is even more true now than it was in 1995.

Reaffirming the tradition of Marx, Engels, Lenin, and Trotsky, the document is also critical of Trotsky on the question of the Stalinist states, like the old USSR.

Some socialists today dismiss that whole debate as yesterday's business. But it is not.

The shadow of Stalinism is there over every conversation we have with people new to politics about what "socialism" is, and how anti-capitalism can avoid falling into Stalinism.

Variant Stalinist systems — Cuba, North Korea — still exist, and still have influence as models.

And on a whole range of questions — some not obvious — the activist left today still sails in a vessel awash with Stalinist seepage from decades past.

The siding of many would-be Marxists with Milosevic's Serbia, or Ahmedinejad's Iran, a stance modelled on the schemes and emotions of the "old" siding with the USSR against "imperialism", is a chief example.

Living in an age of apostasy to socialism and Marxism, and of a great

turning of backs on the past, it is necessary for us to publicly identify and proclaim our roots and traditions.

1. We are Marxists: that is, we believe that Marx was right in his fundamental analysis of capitalist society as a regime of wage slavery; in his analysis of the roots of capitalist exploitation; in his understanding of the class struggle as the locomotive of history; in his identification of the proletariat, the slave class of capitalist society, as the bearer of a new and higher civilisation: "The emancipation of the working class must be conquered by the working class itself"; "The emancipation of the working class is also the emancipation of all human beings without distinction of race and sex."

2. We are Leninists: that is, we believe that the October Revolution was one of the greatest liberating events in human history, and that all socialists who came after that revolution must learn, critically assess, and reassess, its lessons, and adapt them to their own conditions. Centrally, these are: that the class struggle is fought on at least three fronts — the economic, political and ideological fronts — and that socialists are effective only if they fight that struggle on all three fronts in the Bolshevik way: consistently, relentlessly, implacably, irreconcilably; that to do this work in the class struggle, socialists organise themselves into a disciplined, educated, democratic collective, guiding themselves by a Marxist theory, constantly examined, assessed and sharpened in the light of working class experience; that because socialist revolution can be the creation only of a roused, active working class, socialists serve the working class by helping it rouse, educate and organise itself; that socialists connect themselves indissolubly to the working class wherever it is to be found, at whatever level it is at, in all the varying conditions — political, social, ideological — in which it is held under the rule of capital; that, because in all conditions, even when they act as a working class vanguard who believe that their propagandising, lesson-drawing and organising work is essential to the class, socialists serve the working class, and therefore can neither substitute themselves for the working class, nor adopt the role of mere passive speculators about future working class activity; that the serious socialists prepare for the class struggle when they are not fighting it, or when it is at a low ebb: without the slow, preparatory work of many years there would have been no working class revolution in 1917.

3. We are Trotskyists: that is, we root ourselves in and endorse the politics of the rearguard of the Russian Revolution, led by Trotsky; we endorse and glory in the Trotskyist movement's fight against Stalinist totalitarianism; its efforts through a long epoch of murderous reaction to help the working class free itself from the crippling and sometimes suicidal limitations placed on it by Stalinist "communism" and by reformism; its ef-

forts after the collapse of the Communist International to rebuild revolutionary working class parties and a new International, organically of the working class; its policies for fighting fascism in pre-Hitler Germany and for consolidating and defending the working class revolution in Republican Spain during the Civil War: in short, we base ourselves on the first four congresses of the Communist International and on the subsequent development of the politics of those congresses by the movement led by Trotsky until his assassination in 1940.

4. Trotsky summarised his approach thus, in 1938:
"To face reality squarely; not to seek the line of least resistance; to call things by their right names; to speak the truth to the masses, no matter how bitter it may be; not to fear obstacles; to be true in little things as in big ones; to base one's programme on the logic of the class struggle; to be bold when the hour for action arrives — these are the rules of the Fourth International." (*The Transitional Programme*)

5. The first manifesto of our tendency (October 1967) defined Trotskyism as we understood it then, and understand it now:
"Trotskyism is the basic Marxist programme of the conquest of power by the international working class. It is the unfalsified programme, method and experience of the Bolshevism of Lenin and Trotsky. It embodies the world experience of the workers' struggles, including the defence and development of Bolshevism by Trotsky and the Left Opposition in battle against the Stalinist counter-revolution in the Soviet Union. Trotskyism is the only developed working class alternative to venal Stalinism and supine Social Democracy. It means reliance on the self-controlling activity of the masses of the working class, which it strives to mobilise on the programme of transitional demands as a bridge to the overthrow of capitalism and the attainment of workers' power. It is the programme of the workers' revolution, organically linked with the practical struggle to aid its development. It is not only a programme, but the struggle to build a revolutionary party to fight for that programme. Its traditions are those of the Bolsheviks and the Left Opposition: workers' democracy, unremitting struggle for theoretical clarity, revolutionary activism, unbending hostility to and struggle against capitalism and those within the labour movement who stand for its continuation."

6. The Trotskyism of Trotsky, like Lenin's Bolshevism out of which it grew, suffered defeat because in that epoch the working class suffered defeat; it is not a final defeat. The malign Stalinist counterfeit of socialism is dead; the Trotskyist tradition is alive because revolutionary socialism is alive and will remain alive until the working class wins the last battle in the struggle with the bourgeoisie: "Until the last bond and debenture

shrivels to ashes on the grave of the last warlord."

7. This is the tradition in which the Alliance for Workers' Liberty has its roots. In an independent history spanning nearly three decades we have on the basis of this tradition, evolved our own distinct AWL tradition. Beginning as adherents of one of the strands of post-Trotsky Trotskyism — that of James P. Cannon — we have critically re-worked and re-evaluated that tradition, supplementing and amending it on both the level of political ideas and organisational practice. We have, over the years moved a long way from our starting point.

8. We were forced to conclude that, though Trotsky's concrete analyses and descriptions of the Stalinist degeneration of the USSR, and of what that means for the working people there, were exact, continuous, accurate and adequate as an account of the USSR — he did not fail to record that Stalinism differed from Hitler "only in its more unbridled savagery" — and though the conclusions he drew for working class politics inside the USSR were adequate and consistently socialist — from 1935 he advocated a new working class revolution to overthrow the political and social rule of the bureaucracy, calling it a political revolution — Trotsky's conceptual framework was first inadequate and finally led him to radically wrong conclusions. We can see now that the designation "degenerated workers' state" made no sense in the 1930s. He himself tentatively acknowledged this at the end, when he accepted the theoretical possibility that the USSR could, while remaining exactly as it was, bureaucratically collectivised property intact, be conceived of as a new form of class society [The USSR in War, September 1939]. He refused to draw that conclusion then only because he believed that the fall of the Stalinist USSR— either to capitalist restoration or workers' revolution — was imminent.

"Stalin testifies to nothing else but the incapacity of the bureaucracy to transform itself into a stable ruling class. Might we not place ourselves in a ludicrous position if we affixed to the Bonapartist oligarchy the nomenclature of a new ruling class just a few years or even a few months prior to its inglorious downfall?"
[In Defence of Marxism]

9. Trotsky bears no responsibility for the often grotesque politics which his "official", "orthodox" would-be followers built on Trotsky's failure in time to draw the conclusions to which everything he wrote pointed, that the USSR was a new form of class society. Had he lived, Trotsky would either have had to reverse and repudiate his entire train of thought, or draw those conclusions. Everything he wrote on Stalinism in his last three years points to the virtual certainty that he would have diagnosed Stalinism as a new form of class society: Trotsky would not have been a post world war

two "Trotskyist" on this question. The politics of the post-Trotsky Trotskyists towards Stalinism is no part of the authentic Trotskyist tradition but a Stalinist excrescence on it.

10. The majority of the would-be post-Trotsky Trotskyists followed Pablo, Mandel and their associates in analysing the Stalinist states as degenerated and deformed "workers' states", socially in advance of, and superior to, capitalism. The USSR, its satellites in Eastern Europe, China etc. were, they believed, "post-capitalist", in transition between capitalism and socialism.

Keeping Trotsky's label for the USSR — "degenerated workers' state" — and adapting it to the whole cluster of Stalinist formations, the post-Trotsky official Trotskyists, assembled behind the "workers' state" label ideas and assessments starkly at variance with those Trotsky expressed in the same terms. Trotsky's label was retained; all his analyses, perspectives and definitions — all the ideas for him encapsulated in that term — were radically changed. The Marxist politics of honestly settling theoretical accounts with the past gave way to the ancient arts of palimpsestry and to the survival techniques of the chameleon. This would be the cause of much obfuscation and confusion.

11. For Trotsky, at the end, the USSR was an unstable, transitional regime; the Stalinist bureaucracy was a "cancerous growth" on the society created by October, not a necessary social organism capable of defending the USSR or of creating the USSR's post-World War Two empire of 90 million people.

In stark contrast to the views Trotsky expressed in the term, "workers' state", Stalinism was seen by Mandel and the post-Trotsky official Trotskyists as stable; as an agency for accumulating and defending the gains of an ongoing world revolution, which, tangibly, was identical with Stalinism itself. Changes could come only by way of reform (Yugoslavia, China) or political revolution (the USSR), not by regression. These were societies 'in transition to socialism', not, as the USSR was for Trotsky, an aberrant, hybrid formation that could not possibly last (and if it lasted, could not continue to be seen as any sort of workers' state). The Stalinist formations were progressive, post-capitalist, on the broad highway of history — unconditionally progressive, not, as Trotsky at the end said of Stalin's nationalised property, "potentially progressive", on condition that the workers overthrew Stalinism.

12. Trotsky had in 1939/40 already recognised "elements of imperialism" in Stalin's foreign policy, and said: 'We were and remain against the seizure of new territories by the Kremlin.' Though the USSR had a vast empire, for Mandel and his friends it was not "imperialist."

13. Stalinism destroyed labour movements and imposed totalitarian regimes on the working class of Czechoslovakia, East Germany, Poland etc., regimes like that of the USSR which Trotsky in 1938 had rightly described as differing from Hitler's regime "only in its more unbridled savagery", but still this was the — deformed — workers' revolution

According to every criterion the labour movement throughout its history had measured by — civil liberties, political democracy, the free existence of labour movements, free press, speech, sexuality — the USSR, China, etc. were at least as much of a regression as Nazism had been. But, because the — totalitarian — state monopolised property, these systems, vis-à-vis capitalism were, for Pablo and Mandel, unconditionally progressive.

14. Does the bureaucracy play a necessary role in production? You could not, on the post-world war two facts, continue to give Trotsky's negative answer, not even for the USSR. If these were workers' states it was not according to Trotsky.

15. Pablo, Mandel and others reinterpreted the ideas of Trotskyism so as to present the expansion of Stalinism and the creation of totalitarian states in large parts of the world as the first stage of the socialist revolution. Despite the crushing of the working class in the Stalinist states, and its quietness in the big capitalist countries, the "world revolution" was continuing to "develop" — albeit, said Mandel and company, in a deformed way. Ernest Mandel became the word-spinning high priest of the vast, unstable and inchoate ideological edifice which grew up around these core ideas in the 40 years before the USSR collapsed.

16. Ernest Mandel and his friends accepted on their rulers' terms, "critically", of course, such systems as Mao's China and Tito's Yugoslavia, and for decades adopted the role of loyal critic, adopting for these Stalinist states the "reform" politics which the Brandlerites, Lovestoneites, ILPers etc. had, for the USSR in the later 30's counterposed to Trotsky's call for a new —"political" — revolution to overthrow the bureaucratic caste. It was twenty years after Mao's victory before Pablo and Mandel's "Fourth International" came out for a working-class "political" revolution in China.

17. For the post-Trotsky official Trotskyists the workers' state label expressed new ideas, not what it had expressed in Trotsky — and new politics, not those of Trotsky. Whose ideas did the term now express? Bruno Rizzi's! Trotsky had polemicised with Bruno Rizzi's acceptance of Stalinism as a stable system of post-capitalist rule by a collectivist new class. In fact, Rizzi — mimicking Fabians such as Bernard Shaw — believed that

Stalinism and fascism were essentially the same, and that — though Trotsky's polemic ignored this aspect of his thought — both were progressive, both transitional between capitalism and socialism, evolving towards socialism; he saw their horrible features — such as Nazi anti-semitism — as mere kinks in an immature but sufficient anti-capitalist consciousness.

By the end of the 40s Official Trotskyism was expressing not Trotsky's but, essentially, Rizzi's — and Bernard Shaw's — ideas about Stalinism in the terminology Trotsky had used to express his radically different ideas.

18. The epigones of Trotsky proclaimed that the survival and expansion of Stalinism meant defeat for Stalin's "Socialism In One Country" and posthumous triumph for Trotsky and his Permanent Revolution. Mao and Ho were Trotsky's legatees, not Stalin's. In fact, this assessment of the Stalinist states and the Stalinist-led world revolution implied acceptance of the essentials of Socialism In One Country.

The point for Trotsky and his comrades, as for all earlier Marxists, was that socialism had to come after advanced capitalism, could not come otherwise. Though the workers might take power in a backward country, socialism could not be built in backwardness. If the revolution did not spread to countries ripe for socialism, it would be doomed. The idea of stable, evolving socialist growth from peripheral backwardness to socialism, in competition with advanced capitalism, was a revival on a gigantic scale of the pre-Marx colony-building utopian socialism of people like Etienne Cabet, who built small socialist colonies, parallel worlds, in the American wilderness in the 1840s. Pablo and Mandel in their "World Congress" documents [*The Rise and Decline of Stalinism* (1954) and *The Decline and Fall of Stalinism* (1957)] vainly chopped logic to hide this. One country? No longer one country! Socialism in isolation? Not isolated now! Etc.

It was the work of religious zealots, reasoning around daft, unquestionable, fixed ideas, not Marxism. The need for it arose because all the "revolutionary" perspectives and hopes of "official" post-Trotsky Trotskyism were spun from the survival, expansion and likely continuing success of "Socialism In One Country", that is, of the USSR, a world power 'in transition to socialism'.

19. Worse than that. In Lenin and Trotsky, as in Marx and Engels, the historical protagonist of the anti-capitalist revolution is the proletariat. The Trotskyism of Trotsky was the revolutionary working class politics and perspectives of the early Communist International minus, deprived of, the working class armies assembled by the Communist International to make the revolution. Stalinism had "captured" and perverted them. Thus the terrible combination in 1930s Trotskyism of acute awareness, accuracy in understanding and prediction — in pre-Hitler Germany, and in Spain for example — combined with the incapacity to affect events of tiny, tiny

groups whose natural identity, like their "constituency", had been stolen.

All Trotsky's "optimistic" hopes and perspectives were premised on the shifts and regroupments in the proletariat and its parties which he worked to bring about. There would be working class self-clarification, self-re-generation and political regroupment in the heat of class struggle. Wrong, certainly. Fantastic, possibly. But Trotsky's was a perspective in which ends — democratic workers' power — and means — working class risings, the creation of soviets — were appropriate to each other.

By contrast, in post-Trotsky official Trotskyism — "Mandelism" — the identification of Stalinism and Stalinist expansion as the "actually exist-ing" unfolding, albeit deformed, workers' revolution led ineluctably to the destruction of all rational notion of ends and means. The 'official Trot-skyist' fetish of nationalised property — which for Marxists is a means, not an end, and by no means a self-sufficient means — took the central question out of rational assessment: Stalinist statification and its alleged working class character was a 'given', something to reason from, not about.

20. When the "Trotskyists" transformed themselves into an epiphe-nomenon — critical, of course — of Stalinism, they thereby became mil-lenarians.

Primitive millenarian sects, often communistic in their desires, have looked to supernatural events like the second coming of Christ, to trans-form the world into an ideal place. They had no notion of ends and means such as the labour movement would develop — action by named human forces for specific goals. In practice, they would look to some bandit, war-lord or lunatic to begin the designated change. Central for our purposes here was their lack of a rational notion of ends and means.

In post-Trotsky Trotskyism, c.1950, both the ends and means of the pro-letarian revolution in the original Trotskyism, as in traditional Marxism, disappear — or are pushed to the far horizon of history. The "world rev-olutionary perspectives", which Mandel wrote and refurbished for suc-cessive world congresses were, though dressed up in the husks of ideas taken from Trotsky and Lenin, now spun around the USSR, not around the proletariat or its methods or its old socialist goals. The protagonist in "the workers' revolution" is, for now, the Stalinist bloc — Mandel's men-tor Raptis-Pablo once speculated that Stalinism would last for centuries — not, as in Trotsky, the working-class, self-clarified and politically re-grouped. The protagonist is the Stalinist state, the "Red" Army, the Chi-nese peasant army. Though "Perspectives" and hopes for bureaucratic reform and for working class democracy are plentiful in Mandel, they are just tagged on.

21. The proletariat may be crushed under regimes akin to fascism but

despite such 'details' this, nevertheless, they said, is the proletarian revolution. "Nationalised economy" conditions and defines all. How could a Chinese peasant army led by declassed intellectuals, be seen, as the "Fourth International" saw it, as a workers' party? By circular logic: only a workers' party could do what the Maoists did, replicating Stalin's USSR. Ergo, this is a workers' party. Rationalising the Stalinist phenomenon, Mandel's Marxism became arid, eyeless scholasticism. Trotsky's ideas of 1940 were turned into their opposite.

22. The point at which millenarianism triumphed can be dated: the Korean War and the belief that the seemingly inevitable World War Three would be a war-revolution, an international civil war. The nuclear Armageddon — albeit with early nuclear weapons — would also be the revolution. The "Red" Army and its Communist Party allies in western Europe would bring working class victory in the looming war-revolution. You could not go much further from the idea of the socialist revolution — protagonist, ends, means — in Trotsky, and in all previous Marxism. When, a decade later, the Posadas wing of Mandel's organisation took to advocating that "the Russian workers' state" start the third world war, because this would accelerate the world revolution, it only brought out the crazy other-worldly millenarian logic with which Mandel's group had replaced the Trotskyism of Trotsky at the time of the so-called third congress of the Fourth International.

23. The tight millenarianist scenario of 1951-3 centred on Stalinism and war as the agency. Eventually that gave place to a looser millenarianism, promiscuous in its ever-changing choice of saviours. Various nationalist forces, plausibly and implausibly assessed, were anointed — though Stalinism always would be central to the "world revolution" perspectives of all the factions — WRP, SWP USA, Morenists, Lambertists — that made up the "Fourth Internationals" of Trotsky's epigones. Trotsky's tradition and Trotsky's political terminology were thus reduced to mere building blocks in scholastic constructions. Ernest Mandel was from his youth the pre-eminent master in this work. He had many imitators and competitors.

24. Of course their adaptation to Stalinism was never uncritical adaptation — those who ceased to be critical ceased to be even nominally Trotskyist — never inner acceptance of it, never a surrender of the idea that the Stalinist states had to be democratised and transformed. But a man like Ernest Mandel used his erudition and his intellectual talents to weave, from the ideas of Lenin and Trotsky, ideological clothing which could be draped on Stalinism to identify it as part of the world revolution of the proletariat. Directly and indirectly, Mandel and his organisation and its ideological splinter groups such as the Lambertists and Healyites over the

years tied large numbers of anti-Stalinist militants into accepting, tolerating or justifying, "critically", Stalinist regimes and aspects of Russian Stalinist imperialism.

25. Mandel especially played a role similar to that of Karl Kautsky two generations earlier, who rationalised, from the point of view of a hollow "orthodox Marxism", what the leaders of the German social democracy and trade unions did. Here Mandel and his friends were worse than Kautsky. Kautsky devised ideological schemes to depict the time-serving activities of a bureaucratised labour movement as an effective drive for working-class liberation; Mandel produced similar rationalisations for totalitarian Stalinist machines, convinced that they embodied the spirit of history and that it was his job to interpret and rationalise for it. Mandel was the Kautsky of "the historic process" itself.

26. And then, fifty years after Trotsky's death, Stalinism collapsed in Europe. It was revealed as nearer to being pre-capitalist than post-capitalist. Far from "defending and extending, in its own distorted way, the gains of the 1917 workers' revolution", Stalinism must be judged historically to have had no relationship to socialism and working-class emancipation but that of a destroyer of labour movements and an enslaver of working classes.

27. In the course of our work the Alliance for Workers' Liberty discovered that there were other Trotskyist traditions paralleling Cannon's, Mandel's, and that of post-Trotsky official Trotskyism, and in conflict with its peculiar positions on Stalinism; traditions — importantly that of Shachtman's Workers' Party — to which our own evolution — on the question of Stalinism and of democratic procedures in our own ranks, for example — has brought us close. We have learned, and intend to go on learning, from the Workers' Party of the 40s and its successor in the '50s, the Independent Socialist League.

28. In essence our moves away from our origins in post-Trotsky "orthodox Trotskyism" have been part of a journey back to Marx's clear doctrines of working class liberation, without the mystifications and confusions generated in post-Trotsky Trotskyism by its identification of Stalinist states, in which a savage system of class exploitation of workers prevailed, with "deformed" working class revolutions.

29. Tradition is never finished so long as an organisation lives; it goes on being lived, reassessed, amended, transmuted, and developed in the life of a political tendency like ours. In sources of ideas and in the examples — negative as well as positive — we learn from, we are both Can-

nonite and Shachtmanite: in our continuing development we are neither: we continue to evolve our own Workers' Liberty tradition.

30. Critically drawing from the experience of the whole current of Trotskyism, in Trotsky's time and after, the Alliance for Workers' Liberty will continue to build up its forces and fight to win influence for Marxism in the labour movement.

31. Proudly proclaiming that we are Marxist, Leninist, Trotskyist, the Alliance for Workers' Liberty asks for the support of those who see the need to combine clear adherence to the great traditions of the working class past with a commitment to open-minded Marxist thinking about that past and about the struggles of the present. In the name of our traditions, the traditions of militant class struggle and honest revolutionary Marxist socialism — the tradition of Marx, Engels, Lenin, Trotsky, Luxemburg, Mehring, Connolly and countless others — we call for the adherence to our ranks of serious socialists, determined to devote, not the spare evenings of dilettantes, but active dedicate lives to the greatest cause in the world — the fight for the liberation of humankind from capitalist wage slavery and all that goes with it.

32. Marxism is the single most precious achievement of the international proletariat. Of course, Marxism is a product in part of working class experience. The continuing experience of the proletariat is its nourishing life blood. Yet Marxism, scientific consciousness, does not arise spontaneously in the working class. Initially, as the Communist Manifesto rightly says, it comes from outside of the proletariat. It is created by members of the enemy class who come over to the working class, Marx, Engels and others, who fuse the early bourgeois scientific economics, German philosophy and French utopian socialism, with the experience of the first mass working class movement, Chartism, to create a new world outlook . A proletarian world outlook.

Marxism, whose adherents analyse, interpret, codify and try to shape an ever changing, evolving, permuting, social world is never 'finished'. It grows and develops, or else — as in many of its sectarian embodiments — it petrifies or withers; and thereby dies. Marxism can not stand still, because social reality does not stand still.

33. The AWL bases itself on Marxism — that is, an awareness of the basic texts and theories, and history of Marxism, together with knowledge of the history of society and of the working class and social movements required to make sense of the codifications that make up Marxism.

One of two things then.

Either: 'Marxism' is the property of the whole organisation, that is, the whole organisation consists of Marxists educated above a high basic level; or Marxism in the organisation is the property of a minority, even a small minority, who form a mere sect inside the organisation. If they are the leadership, they assume the role of a priestly cast in relation to the rest of the organisation's members. It is a pre-requisite of a healthy Marxist organisation, that everybody knows the basics; that, up to a high minimum, everybody is able to understand what is going on, what the ramifications and implications of the issues raised are.

If a basic minimum education is not a condition of participation of the organisation's deliberations, that is, of membership in the Marxist organisation, then inequality is built into the organisation, and into its system of recruitment and induction. So is the potential of the emergence of a priestly caste, and of the corruption of the organisation's internal life by demagogy ; and, even as in the case of SWP, of the suppression of all real internal political life in the organisation.

34. A feature of most of the kitsch-Trotskyist sects is that in them there is a priestly caste, with an unhealthy, manipulative relationship to the membership.

The SWP which is a mutant strain of kitsch-Trotskyism is one of the clearest examples. Even when it was an open, more or less democratic organisation, 'theory' was the property of a small elite of bourgeois intellectuals, and not even minimally — on such a thing, for example, as the group's fetishised theory of state capitalism — the property of the membership. We criticised them at the time, for that and for the crude and manipulative demagogy that served the priestly caste to mediate between their theory and the rank and file of the organisation. They did not, we said, understand what theory was for in a revolutionary organisation; that either it was a real guide to cogitations, discussions and decisions by all the members of the party, or else that the organisation could not be a functioning Marxist collective at all. We said with tragic accuracy, before it occurred, that this state of affairs would inevitably lead to the degeneration of the organisation (see documents reprinted in *International Communist* No.5 1977).

35. There will of course, unavoidably, always be different levels of understanding and of learning in any organisation; and then again different levels within any leading committee. Some people will know and understand more, and contribute more in the common deliberations. A serious Marxist organisation has no tolerance for denial of this, or for demagogic pseudo-workerist demands for levelling down — no one has a right to know more, or if they know it, to express more than us poor workers can effortlessly understand — of the sort the — essentially petit bourgeois — Thornettites once made notorious in our ranks. The Marxist movement

levels up, not down.

The serious Marxist organisation will normally insist on a process of recruitment and induction where the aspirant member is put through a basic minimum education in Marxism, and does not acquire full rights inside the organisation until such an education is completed. In conditions of major working class upsurge we would of course recruit more loosely. We can only do that with safety to our basic identity and security for our political integrity when:

i. There is already a properly educated cadre

ii. and when that cadre understands that one of its cardinal functions is to educate the militants recruited in the heat of the class struggle. Thus it was with the Bolshevik Party in 1905-7, and again in 1917.

Any organisation trying — as organisations like the AWL must — to function as a collective, able to analyse the world as Marxists while making propaganda for Marxism inside the labour movement, and in the class struggle, will suffer a number of terrible, and ultimately self destroying, consequences if it recruits too loosely and neglects education.

• Printed in *Workers' Liberty* 3-27, January 2010

What was the Minority Movement?

By Stan Crooke

Taking its name from a union bureaucrat's complaint about a "minority of troublemakers", the National Minority Movement (NMM) was formally established in August 1924 as a rank-and-file trade union organisation.

The founding conference was attended by over 270 delegates, claiming to represent some 200,000 workers. It defined the "aims and objects" of the NMM as:

"To organise the working masses of Great Britain for the overthrow of capitalism, the emancipation of the workers from oppressors and exploiters, and the establishment of a Socialist Commonwealth.

"To carry on a wide agitation and propaganda for the principles of revolutionary class struggle... and against the present tendency towards social peace and class collaboration, and the delusion of the peaceful transition from capitalism to socialism."

Between its founding conference in 1924 and the General Strike of 1926 the NMM grew substantially. 443 delegates attended its 1925 conference, and 547 delegates attended the following year's conference.

At its height, the NMM claimed to represent 957,000 workers. Unfortunately, the real figure was a lot lower: a union branch's membership would be counted three times over if the branch itself, the local union district committee, and the local Trades Council all sent delegates to a NMM conference.

Moreover, support for the NMM was very unevenly spread, both in terms of unions and geographically.

Only amongst miners, engineers and, to a much lesser degree, transport workers did the NMM enjoy a solid base of support. Geographically, support for the NMM was concentrated primarily in London, Sheffield, and parts of Scotland and Wales.

Yet the early years of the NMM are an important source of lessons — both positive and negative — for revolutionaries in our trade union work.

The driving force behind the NMM was the Communist Party of Great Britain (CPGB), founded in 1921 as the product of the fusion of a number of small socialist organisations. It was a revolutionary party.

Modelling itself (even if not always successfully) on Lenin's Bolshevik Party which had achieved victory in Russia, the CPGB embodied a new approach to the struggle for revolutionary politics.

Prior to the CPGB's foundation, most socialist organisations in this country had been propagandistic: instead of actively intervening in the class struggle, they made passive propaganda about the need for socialism.

Their approach to politics is summed up by the following description of their public meetings (which were usually their only form of public activity):

"The speeches usually took the form of a general statement of socialist aspirations, a general criticism of capitalism and its evils, and a special application to current happenings — particularly the doings of the local borough or town council."

Consequently, such socialist organisations took little interest in the trade unions and workers' industrial struggles. The only exception to this was the Socialist Labour Party (SLP), which did have a major orientation to workplace struggles.

But the SLP suffered from a major weakness of its own: syndicalism. It believed that strike action and industrial union organisation alone would be enough to achieve socialism.

This fundamental difference between the CPGB and its predecessors was summed up by JT Murphy, a leading figure in both the CPGB and also the NMM, after attending an international congress of Communist Parties in 1920:

"Instead of thinking that a socialist party was merely a propaganda organisation for the dissemination of socialist views, I now saw that a real socialist party would consist of revolutionary socialists who regarded the party as a means whereby they would lead the working class in the fight for political power."

This new insight into the nature and role of the revolutionary party underpinned the CPGB's approach to work in the unions.

Party members were not to be a mere "ginger group" in the unions, pushing union leaders to the left. Their task was to mobilise workers on the basis of class struggle politics as part of the fight to achieve a revolutionary leadership of the workers' movement.

Sectarian and syndicalist prejudices had not been completely eliminated amongst the party membership. As one party member later recalled:

"Considerable time and energy had to be expended to fight down the belief that there was no room for a movement dealing with immediate and 'narrow' economic issues, that it was a reformist conception.

"(Some members believed) that such an organisation would stand in front of and hide the face of the Party from the workers. Sneering descriptions of the NMM were given in the Party as being 'an attempt to dress a red man in a pink cloak'."

There was thus a constant tension in the trade union work of the CPGB in the early to mid 1920s and, by extension, the NMM itself.

Another, far more powerful, influence was at work as well. The CPGB looked to Moscow for political guidance. As Stalin consolidated his grip on power in the Soviet Union, the political guidance which the CPGB received was based increasingly upon class collaboration rather than class confrontation.

Early years of the Minority Movement

But in 1924 the NMM signalled a new approach. It opened up the possibility of united action by CPGB members and union militants outside the ranks of the party in a joint struggle against both the capitalists and also the "labour lieutenants of capital" in the union bureaucracy.

As NMM National Secretary Pollitt put it: "It was necessary to make a decisive turn towards mass work in the factories, trade unions and working-class organisations, and to try to end the old sectarian traditions of the British revolutionary movement once and for all."

The CPGB had already begun such an approach prior to the creation of the NMM as a national organisation.

In 1922 the party had taken the lead in organising a series of "Back to the Unions" conferences as part of its "Stop the Retreat" campaign. The aim was to reverse the fall in union membership resulting from the employers' offensive and from the repeated betrayals by trade union leaders.

In the early years of the NMM, particular emphasis was placed upon the creation of powerful Trades Councils which would function as local general staffs of the working class: "By joint activities of the unions and Trades Councils (we can) create powerful nuclei around which the masses will gather."

The NMM campaigned for all union branches and district committees to affiliate to Trades Councils, and also called for a change in the structures of Trades Councils: they should accept direct workshop representation, and their right to send delegates to TUC congresses should be restored.

Affiliation to the National Federation of Trades Councils (initiated by the CPGB in 1923) was another campaigning focus of the NMM. As a result of such initiatives, the NMM itself won the affiliation of over 50 Trades Councils in the period 1924-26.

Arguably, the CPGB overestimated the potential of Trades Councils. And by the time of the General Strike it was certainly using its influence to ensure Trades Councils meekly fell into line behind the TUC.

Even so, there is some basis in reality for the NMM's claim that it was "the first organised movement… to draw attention to the importance and real role of Trades Councils in the labour movement."

Similar considerations apply to the NMM's call for increased powers for the TUC General Council. The political validity of this demand should not be obscured by the later failure of the NMM to challenge the role played by the General Council in the General Strike.

Well before the establishment of the CPGB many militants and socialists had advocated greater powers for the TUC General Council and its transformation into a "general staff of labour."

The concentration of capital demanded that the labour movement should concentrate its forces and break away from trade union sectionalism. As one NMM pamphlet put it, a TUC "General Staff" would:

"Mobilise and concentrate all the forces of the working class movement for the purpose of opposing a united class front to the united capitalist enemy... Sectional fighting is doomed, only conscious class fighting can be of use."

But the CPGB and NMM did, at least initially, recognise that increased powers for the General Council could be used to police the union membership in the interests of capitalism, unless those powers were subject to rank-and-file control and were used in pursuit of the class struggle.

This was clearly spelt out in a resolution passed at the NMM's founding conference. If the General Council was to become a "Workers' General Staff" rather than a "machine of the capitalists", what was necessary was:

"In the first place and fundamentally, to develop a revolutionary class consciousness amongst the trade union membership, and in the second place to so alter the constitution of the General Council as to ensure that those elected thereon have the closest contact with the workers."

"All power to the General Council"

Before long, however, the qualifications and safeguards linked to the demand for increased powers for the General Council slipped into the background, and then out of sight, in the agitation of the CPGB and the NMM.

The 1925 conference of the NMM, for example, again called for more powers for the General Council, but added only as a vague afterthought that such powers should be used "to fight more effectively the battles of the workers."

The CPGB itself collapsed into wishful thinking: "The new General Council (of 1925) will simply have to prosecute more vigorously the fight on behalf of the workers... The mass pressure from behind will force even then (the right-wingers on the General Council) to toe the line."

Hardy, a leading figure in the NMM, displayed a similar attitude of political blindness when questioned about the wisdom of the slogan "All power to the General Council" in March 1926:

"Should they use that power wrongly, it only means that we have got another additional task before us of forcing them in the right direction, which direction they will ultimately have to take."

By the time of the General Strike itself, two months later, the CPGB had completely turned its back on its earlier understanding of how to raise the question of increased powers for the General Council. Now the role of the CPGB was to be a dogsbody:

"Our party does not hold the leading position in the trade unions. It is not conducting the negotiations with the employers and the government. It can only advise and place its forces at the service of the workers — led by others."

With the NMM's campaigning for industrial unionism and workshop committee too, positive initiatives foundered on the rocks of deference to the union bureaucracy.

From its founding conference onwards, the NMM campaigned to reorganise trade unions so that each industry was represented by one union. Divisions between workers in different unions in the same industry could thus be broken down.

The achievement of industrial unions, a long-standing objective of revolutionaries and syndicalists well before the creation of the NMM, would help bring about a unified workers' movement and thereby strengthen the forces of labour in the class struggle.

Campaigning for industrial unionism meant an emphasis on campaigning at rank-and-file level. This had been recognised by the unofficial shop stewards' movement during the 1914-18 war. It always emphasised that "unity from below" was the precondition of industrial unionism.

In practice, however, the NMM looked increasingly towards the TUC and the union executives to bring about industrial unionism.

Thus, a resolution passed by the 1924 TUC, originating from the Minority Movement in the South Wales Miners Federation, instructed the TUC itself to "draw up a scheme of organisation by industry."

Needless to say, the General Council allowed the resolution to remain a dead letter. The minutes of the following year's TUC record the lament of one CPGB member who attended the Congress as a union delegate:

"…Delegates' confusion was made worse and confounded by the General Council not giving any lead whatever. He suggested that the General Council might have done something to resuscitate the enthusiasm which had been engendered in the workshops."

The NMM did not completely transform the proposals for industrial unionism and workshop committees into appeals for implementation by the bureaucracy. In 1926, for example, the NMM press was itself advocating that rank-and-file trade unionists take the initiative in setting up workplace committees.

Even so, there had been a clear drift on the part of the NMM — away from action and initiative at rank-and-file level, and towards appeals for industrial unionism and workshop committees under the patronage of the TUC.

Writing in the CPGB's newspaper in 1926, Hardy merely listed the more militant resolutions passed at the previous year's TUC congress as proof of the positive achievements of the NMM. This was completely at odds with the role originally envisaged for the NMM.

In the General Strike

The crucial test for the NMM came in the run-up to the General Strike of May 1926. The conflicting tendencies which had always been apparent in the NMM, and the CPGB, reached a climax.

Organisationally, the NMM survived the General Strike. Politically, the NMM irrevocably turned its back on the revolutionary politics which had inspired its creation. The NMM survived the General Strike in name only.

A special conference of the NMM held in March 1926 agreed upon a plan of action in preparation for the looming General Strike.

Particular emphasis was placed upon the formation of Councils of Action in the localities. Without waiting for the TUC General Council to give a lead, the NMM circulated all Trades Councils with an appeal to call Conferences of Action:

"Conferences of Action (should be convened) for the purpose of setting up Councils of Action under the control and auspices of the Trades and Labour Councils."

The Councils of Action were to bring together representatives from working-class political and trade union organisations, and also from the unemployed workers' movement. Their role was to prepare for taking over the running of essential services during the General Strike.

The NMM conference also advocated the establishment of a Workers' Defence Corps, the formation of workshop committees, and the extension of the Triple Alliance, "with instructions given to the General Council to take over the leadership of the alliance on behalf of the whole working class movement."

In response to the national appeal of the NMM and the work of NMM members in the localities, many Trades Councils did convene Unity of Action Conferences for the purpose of establishing Councils of Action.

During the General Strike these Councils organised mass meetings, produced local strike bulletins, mobilised workers for mass pickets, and, in some areas, established Workers' Defence Corps and took over the control of essential services.

Well over 1,000 CPGB members — some 25% of the organisation's membership — were arrested for their activities during the General Strike. The entire top leadership of the CPGB had already been arrested the previous year and, not by chance, was still in prison at the time of the General Strike.

There can be no doubt about the commitment of members of the NMM and the CPGB to the miners' cause and a working-class victory in the General Strike. The tragedy was that the NMM and the CPGB proved incapable of providing effective leadership during the run-up to the strike and the strike itself.

In 1925 the CPGB had correctly argued that, "the miners' crisis is part of the general economic crisis in British industrialism. It has passed beyond any purely economic stage. It is a definitely political crisis and can only be solved by revolutionary political means."

But by the eve of the General Strike the CPGB had struck a very different note:

"To entertain any exaggerated views as to the revolutionary possibilities of this crisis and visions of a new leadership 'arising spontaneously in the struggle' etc., is fantastic."

This about-turn was equally noticeable in relation to the fake-lefts on the TUC General Council — the bureaucrats who talked left but acted right.

Shortly after the formation of the NMM, J. R. Campbell, a leading figure in the CPGB, had warned:

"It would be a suicidal policy for the CP and the NMM to place too much reliance on the official left wing. It is the duty of the Party and the NMM to criticise its weakness relentlessly."

In the run-up to the General Strike the political bankruptcy of the fake-lefts became daily more apparent. They did nothing to implement the left-wing resolutions passed by the 1925 TUC Congress, and they made no preparations for the General Strike.

But neither the CPGB nor the NMM set about criticising their weaknesses relentlessly. Instead, they merely complained about the "lack of self-confidence" of the fake-lefts, and urged them to "overcome their weaknesses." They had "acted very foolishly" and needed to show more determination in future.

When the fake-lefts duly betrayed the General Strike, many CPGB members were genuinely confused by the behaviour of "our friends on the General Council." As one CPGB member plaintively asked:

"Why did the better and more virile members of the General Council — those we have called the 'Left Wing' — allow themselves to become involved in their [i.e. the right-wingers'] panic?"

The role envisaged for the Councils of Action who underwent a dramatic transformation between 1925 and 1926.

In 1925, when a General Strike seemed possible in July, the Councils of Action were to take the lead in spreading the strike action, organising mass demonstrations and mass picketing, and fighting for an unofficial general strike.

By 1926, however, the leaders of the NMM and the CPGB were declaring that:

"There should be no rival body to the Trades Council... We should avoid rivalry and recognise the General Council as the General Staff of the unions, directing the unions in the struggle."

The NMM had been set up to fight for the revolutionary transformation of the trade union movement. But less than two years after its creation it was spinning illusions in fake-lefts and calling on workers to fall into line behind the TUC General Council.

The influence of Stalin

The reasons for this degeneration lie partly in the significance attached to the maintenance of the Anglo-Russian Trade Union Committee (ARTUC) by the CPGB.

The ARTUC was a bloc between the emerging Stalinist regime in the Soviet Union and the British TUC. Having abandoned any commitment to promoting international socialist revolution, Stalin looked to international diplomacy and alliances with labour movement bureaucracies abroad in order to "protect" the Soviet Union.

The fake-lefts were leading supporters of the ARTUC, formally established in 1925: it boosted their fake-left credentials. The CPGB, as loyal followers of Stalin, was therefore anxious not to alienate the fake-lefts, in case this led to them pulling out of the ARTUC.

But this factor can be only a partial explanation for the degeneration of the NMM.

The NMM and the CPGB had been inconsistent in their attitude towards the union bureaucracy before the creation of the ARTUC. Criticism of the union bureaucracy, for example, had been largely confined to the theoretical publications of the CPGB and had been less than prominent in the party's agitational press. On the other hand, the NMM and the CPGB were criticised by Moscow for their softness towards the bureaucracy even after the ARTUC had been set up.

The NMM conference of 1926, for example, held after the defeat of the General Strike, advocated that members restrain criticism of the TUC General Council where it was likely to "militate against the possibilities of bringing the miners' strike to a successful conclusion or operate against the future welfare of Anglo-Russian unity."

This position was sharply rebuked by Moscow. Instead of soft-peddling its criticisms, the NMM should recognise that "merciless criticism and exposure of the manoeuvres of the new consolidated trade union bureaucracy is one of the foremost tasks in the struggle for the revolutionising of the British trade union movement."

How sincere Moscow was in its appeal to revolutionise the British unions is, to put it mildly, open to debate. Clearly, though, there was an internal dynamic to the increasingly erratic course pursued by the NMM in 1925/6.

The shortcomings and eventual degeneration of the NMM were rooted in the failure of the CPGB, the driving political force in the NMM, to overcome the political legacy which it had inherited from its political predecessors.

That legacy was mainly one of propagandism and syndicalism, sometimes accompanied by opportunism. In its early years the CPGB, under the guidance of a genuinely revolutionary movement based in Moscow, had begun to overcome that legacy. The formation of the NMM itself was one manifestation of this.

But the CPGB never completely broke from its political inheritance. Syndicalism remained a force within it, as too did the opportunism of some of its members who had previously belonged to the British Socialist Party.

The CPGB's level of theoretical and political training was insufficient to eradicate such political shortcomings. As JT Murphy put it in 1924:

"If I were asked what are the principal defects of the Party today, I would answer unhesitatingly: formalism, organisational fetishism, and lack of political training."

Once the pressure from Moscow ceased to correct the failings of the CPGB — and instead hardened out such failings into a political method — the CPGB and the NMM collapsed into political incoherence.

On the positive side, in its early period, the NMM displayed a real drive to carry the struggle for revolutionary politics into the workers' movement. It did not dismiss the trade unions as reformist, but regarded them as a vital arena of struggle.

And negatively, in terms of its degeneration and eventual demise, the NMM taught an even more valuable lesson: a socialist who lacks a coherent revolutionary world-view is incapable of effective intervention in the trade unions.

• From *Workers' Liberty* 32, June 1996

ISSUES FOR THE LEFT
The truth about BDS

By Harry Glass

The boycott, divestment, and sanctions (BDS) campaign has become the dominant frame for viewing the Israel-Palestine conflict in recent years and Omar Barghouti has been its most high-profile exponent.

His book Boycott, Divestment, Sanctions: The Global Struggle for Palestinian Rights (Haymarket Books) demonstrates the real political confusion behind BDS and why socialists should oppose it.

The BDS campaign dates from 9 July 2005, when a gathering of 170 Palestinian organisations, including unions and civil society groups demanded boycott, divestment, and sanctions against Israel. BDS makes three demands on Israel:

• ending the occupation and colonisation of all Arab lands [occupied in 1967] and dismantling the wall;

• recognising the fundamental rights of the Arab-Palestinian citizens of Israel to full equality;

• respecting, protecting and promoting the rights of Palestinians refugees to return to their homes and properties.

These are often dressed in the garb of UN resolutions. The first two demands are completely reasonable for any democrat or socialist. However there are fundamental problems with the demand for the right of return.

First and foremost, it is a slippery formula, evasive about who it applies to — is it simply those displaced in 1948 or all Palestinians, does it mean the same place they were living then, or simply immigration into a new Palestinian state? Ultimately the demand is incoherent with regard to the political basis of a democratic solution to Israeli-Palestinian relations. The BDS campaign publicly fudges the question of the political solution. Officially "the BDS movement as such does not adopt any special political formula and steers away from the one-state-versus-two-states debate".

However Barghouti is quite explicit about his view. He states: "I have for over twenty-five years consistently supported the secular democratic unitary state solution in historic Palestine". He laments that now "there is no political party in Palestine now or among Palestinians in exile calling for a secular, democratic state solution". His politics are the PLO's, frozen in 1987.

Barghouti is also unequivocally opposed to a two states solution. He says: "The two-state solution is not only impossible to achieve now — Israel has made it an absolute pipe dream that cannot happen — but also, crucially, an immoral solution. At best it would address some of the rights of Palestinians in the occupied West Bank and Gaza, a mere one-third of the Palestinian people".

But in a moment of candour, he reveals that the political basis of BDS is not compatible with two states either. He wrote: "You cannot practically reconcile the right of return for refugees with a negotiated two-state solution". There it is in black and white: support BDS and you are tied to a single state solution.

Barghouti offers an impoverished version of self-determination. He moralises that "A call signed by more than 170 Palestinian political parties, unions, nongovernmental organisations, and networks, representing the entire spectrum of Palestinian civil society... cannot be 'counterproductive' unless Palestinians are not rational or intelligent enough to know or articulate what is in their best interest".

He also says no Palestinian party stands for a single state — but there is no need to defer to that opinion! So 170 organisations call for boycott; but no-one is for his real objective — secular, democratic state. Too bad for the Palestinians — they can be trusted with the means, but not the end. He reduces Palestinian oppression to racial rather than national terms, hence all the rhetoric about apartheid.

On the other side, Barghouti simply denies that Israeli Jews have any right to self determination at all. He cannot conceptualise them as a nation, therefore their self determination is not even discussed. He sugarcoats his "solution", saying he wants "a secular democratic state where nobody is thrown into the sea, nobody is sent back to Poland, and nobody is left suffering in refugee camps".

Yet there is no explicit criticism of Hamas in the book. He simply dismisses the problem of Hamas' politics altogether: "It's irrelevant whether or not Hamas accepts Israel's so-called right to exist as a Jewish state (read: an apartheid state) or accepts the '67 borders ...".

With the single state solution, whether secular or Islamic, neither the Palestinians nor the Israelis get to exercise their own, self-defined, self-determination.

Barghouti's failure to engage with the right of Israeli Jews to self-determination is clear from his contempt for the Israeli left. "...most of what passes as 'left' in Israel are Zionist parties and groups that make some far-right parties in Europe look as moral as Mother Teresa". And "The so-called peace groups in Israel largely work to improve Israeli oppression against the Palestinians, rather than eliminate it, with their chief objective being the guarantee of Israel's future as a 'Jewish' — that is, exclusivist — state. The most radical Israeli 'Zionist-left' figures and groups are still

Zionist, adhering to the racist principles of Zionism that treat the indigenous Palestinians as lesser humans who are the obstacle or a 'demographic threat'..."

Barghouti explicitly defames those who argue that the logic of the right of return would be the elimination of the state of Israel: "the only true fighters for peace in Israel are those who support our three fundamental rights: the right of return for Palestinian refugees; full equality for the Palestinian citizens of Israel and ending the occupation and colonial rule".

Laughably, Barghouti states that the BDS movement "does not subscribe to drawing up lists to decide who is a good Israeli and who is not based on some arbitrary political criteria". Yet this is precisely what he does. He narrows progressive Israelis to only those who support BDS – eliminating for example the refuseniks, the peace movement, the unions and various writers. All the rest are branded with inverted commas.

Barghouti is quite upfront that BDS ultimately means ostracising everything Israeli. The campaign is "working to expel Israel and its complicit institutions from international and interstate academic, cultural, sporting... environmental, financial, trade, and other forums." He soft-soaps that "groups that for tactical reasons support only a subset of BDS, or a targeted boycott of specific products or organisations in Israel, or supporting Israel, are still our partners. Boycott is not a one-size-fits-all type of process."

He distinguishes between advocating such a targeted boycott as a tactic, leading to the ultimate goal of boycotting all Israeli goods and services, and advocating such a targeted boycott as the ultimate strategy. While the former "may be necessary in some countries as a convenient and practical tool to raise awareness and promote debate about colonial and apartheid regime, the latter, despite its lure, would be in direct contradiction with the stated objectives of the Palestinian boycott movement".

For Barghouti the boycott of settlement goods alone is not sufficient. At a practical level "Israel has made it extremely difficult to differentiate between settlement and other Israeli products, simply because the majority of parent companies are based inside Israel or because colony-based companies have official addresses there".

Politically "even if distinguishing between produce of settlements and produce of Israel were possible, activists who on principle — rather than out of convenience — advocate a boycott of only the former may argue that they are merely objecting to the Israeli military occupation and colonisation of 1967 and have no further problems with Israel".

Finally, there is a moral problem with accepting these "two grave... violations of human rights and international law as givens".

BDS may seem in the ascendant for now. It may make progress in places, on the back of the Israeli state's next atrocity. But BDS needs to be fought politically, because it stands in the path of two states, the only consistently democratic solution to the Israel-Palestine conflict.

BDS is ultimately a pessimistic approach. It put the agency for change outside of the region. It wants civil society, which includes not only NGOs and unions but bourgeois governments and business internationally, to make things right for the Palestinians. There is another road. The Palestinian workers in alliance with Israeli workers fighting for a two state democratic solution to the national question, is the force that could deliver peace and much more besides.

• From *Solidarity* 211, 8 July 2011

What is the Muslim Brotherhood?

The Socialist Workers Party called for a vote for the Muslim Brotherhood in the second round of the 2012 Egyptian Presidential elections. In extracts from two articles *Clive Bradley* assesses the history and political character of the first Islamist group.

It was in Egypt that the first Islamist organisation was founded — the Society of Muslim Brothers, by Hassan al-Banna in 1928. Arguably the early Muslim Brotherhood was closer to traditional Islamic revivalism than to modern Islamism, but in any case its history flows directly and continuously into that modern Islamism.

Egypt at the time was a British protectorate ruled by an unpopular king. The nationalist movement (principally the Wafd Party) was militant, but had proved unsuccessful, and was thoroughly bourgeois, making little effort to mobilise its popular support around social questions. The Muslim Brothers began as a conservative movement for social reform, aiming to encourage Egyptians — and later Muslims elsewhere — to rediscover their Islamic heritage and behave like proper believers. Its base, like that of later Islamist groups, was among the urban middle class, the "effendis".

Gradually al-Banna's organisation moved in a more overtly political direction. In the 1936-39 Arab revolt against Jewish settlers and British rulers in Palestine, they sent fighters. They played a part in making the question of Palestine, even at that early stage, an "Arab" or regional issue. At the same time, the Brothers moved further towards armed, terrorist-type action.

They had an uneasy relationship with the nationalist parties, but by the late 1940s, when al-Banna was assassinated, had developed a considerable base.

In 1952 the Free Officers overthrew the king and kicked out the British. Some of them had links with the Brothers. For a short while the Brothers supported, and even took part in, the new government. But they were hostile to the land reform which broke the power of the landlords, and quite soon the Brothers found themselves under arrest and facing persecution. As the regime became more radical, and began to introduce "Arab socialism" [state ownership], the Brothers opposed such atheistic heresy. They faced intense repression, along with other oppositional forces like the Communist Party. In the mid-60s, accused of an attempt on Nasser's life, thousands of them were rounded up.

One of those arrested, and executed along with other leaders of the movement in 1966, was Sayyid Qutb, who was probably the real intellectual founder of modern militant Islamism, at least in those lands where the Sunni (more Protestant-like) version of Islam dominates rather than the minority Shi'a (more Catholic-like) version centred in Iran.

Qutb developed his distinctive ideas after the Egyptian Ministry of Education, for which he worked as an official, sent him to the USA in 1948-51 to study American methods of schooling. He returned to Egypt with an uncompromising hatred for the West and all its works. Qutb's rejection of the West was not that of the conservative concerned with preserving his culture's traditions against foreign encroachments, but rather that of the 'born-again Muslim' who having adopted or absorbed many modern influences makes a show of discarding them in his search for personal identity and cultural authenticity.

After his arrest, Qutb wrote his famous work, *Signposts,* which is the first clear statement of the aims and worldview of the sects we now think of as Islamist, and is required reading for the cadre of these groups. Qutb defined the regime itself as part of the "infidel" problem. Society was divided into the Party of God and the Party of Satan. The Islamist movement was surrounded by a swamp of ignorance and unbelief (jahiliyya, the term used to describe the society of Arabia before the coming of Muhammed). The creation of an Islamic government was not just a culturally preferable alternative, but a divine imperative. The method of creating it would be jihad, or holy war. (For some Muslims, jihad can mean private spiritual striving, but for Islamist groups it increasingly means, very literally, war.) It is unclear if Qutb himself would have wholeheartedly approved of the modern groups who claim his legacy; but he spelled out the main themes of modern militant Islamism.

As Sadat moved away from Nasserist state-capitalism in the 1970s, the Muslim Brothers re-emerged from their eclipse by repression. Sadat was initially warm towards them. He had broken with the USSR; his new economic policy was unpopular, and opening up dangerous space on his left (both within the regime and outside it). The Brothers were a useful counterbalance. More, Sadat flirted considerably with using Islam as a source of legitimacy as Nasserist ideology was put out to grass: he made much of his own commitment to the faith, and introduced Islamic laws — stoking communal antagonism between Muslims and Egypt's extremely large Christian minority.

The Brothers were still technically illegal, but they grew in the 1970s. And more radical schisms began to emerge. A group called the Islamic Liberation Organisation attempted a coup in 1974, seizing the Technical

Military Academy in Cairo. The ILO had links with other Islamist groups abroad. In January 1973 it had published its manifesto, which claims, for instance:

"Liberation is a means, not an end... When we fight for the liberation of Palestine, we do not fight... for the sake of getting back our homeland, but for the glorification of the word of God... We fight to transform every Dar al-kufr [reign of unbelief] into Dar al-Islam, whether its people are Muslims as in Pakistan, or infidels as in India."

A better known group, Takfir wa Hijra (roughly, Atonement and Exile — hijra refers to Mohammed's leaving Mecca for Medina), assassinated a teacher at al-Azhar, Cairo's prestigious mosque-university, who was also minister for religious endowments. When Sadat made peace with Israel, signing a peace treaty in 1978 at Camp David, he had effectively signed his own death warrant. The militant group al-Jihad had formed cells in the army. In 1981, as Sadat was admiring his troops on the anniversary of the 1973 war, Khaled Islambouli shot him dead.

There followed a period of intense upheaval. Islamists in the town of Asyut, where they were strong, attempted an uprising which was crushed. The new regime of Hosni Mubarak began to arrest, imprison and torture Islamists or suspected Islamists in huge numbers — thousands of them — a tradition it has continued ever since.

Chukri Mustapha, an agricultural engineer considered the "emir", or leader, of Takfir wa Hijra, expressed his ideology thus:

"God be praised. He will prepare the land for the group of the just by provoking a war between the two great powers, Russia and America... The war is inevitable, they will destroy each other. God will thus have prepared the land for the Islamic state... Following [this war] the forces of the Muslim nation will be about equal to those of its enemies. It is then that the true Jihad will start.'

As the gama'at islamiyya, the militant groups, began to grow, the Muslim Brothers moved more into the mainstream. By the end of the 70s, they had formally declared their abandonment of terrorist activity. By the late 80s, although unable to stand in elections, they formed electoral pacts, first with the Wafd, then with the so-called Socialist Labour Party (getting 17% of the vote in 1987). More importantly, they established a network of schools, clinics, and even banks — a pattern typical of Islamist movements — and made huge inroads into Egypt's professional associations, mainly among engineers, doctors, and by the late 90s, lawyers, winning a majority in the bar association. The Brothers, in other words, sank deep social roots, with cadres in the urban middle class and support from the unorganised poor. In student bodies, too, both moderate and militant Islamists have grown. Now the Brothers are the best-organised and chief opposition to the Mubarak government. In an attempt to curtail their influence, in addition to repression, the state tried to extend its control over mosques;

but there are simply too many of these for such control to be effective.

Moderate and legalistic as they now are, it should not be thought that the Brothers are a benign force in Egyptian political life. When the Muslim academic Nasr Abu Zaid put forward a theory that the Qur'an was read and interpreted differently according to historical context, the Brothers declared him an apostate, drove him from the university, and tried, through the courts, to force his wife to divorce him. The couple fled to Scandinavia.

The weight of the moderate, "reformist" Brothers provides the ideological context for the radical variants. Those grew increasingly violent. In the 1990s, the militant groups made a turn to assassinating tourists, beginning with the murder of some Israelis in Sinai, and tourists near the pyramids. Then in 1997, an attack was launched at the ancient temple of Hatshepsut at Luxor which left 68 tourists and three Egyptians dead. Other murders have been carried out of Coptic Christians; the Nobel Prize winning author Neguib Mahfuz was stabbed; the outspoken secular journalist Farag Fuda was murdered.

Tala'at Fu'ad Qassim, of the Egyptian Islamist group Gama'a Islamiyya, justified the murder of tourists like this:

"[Tourism]... is a means by which prostitution and AIDS are spread by Jewish women tourists, and it is a source of all manner of depravities, not to mention being a means of collecting information on the Islamic movement. For these reasons we believe tourism is an abomination which must be destroyed. And it is one of our strategies for destroying the government."

Indeed, these attacks crippled Egypt's tourism industry, one of its chief sources of income and foreign exchange. Qassim's group, like Islamic Jihad, has strong links in Afghanistan; Ayman al-Zawahiri of al-Jihad was bin Laden's supposed "deputy". Al-Jihad seemed to be the largest of the militant groups, building up influence in slum areas through study groups, distributing literature and audio cassettes with Islamic speeches, providing welfare services, and so on.

A truce was declared between the Islamists and Mubarak's government in 1997. Several thousand detainees were released, although 12,000 or so Islamists remained in prison. After 11 September 2001, though, a new clampdown began.

• From a much longer article 'The rise of political Islam', *Workers' Liberty* 2-2

The Brotherhood's dominant characteristic since the 1970s has been "moderate". Moderate means what? It means, most obviously, the renunciation of armed struggle. The Brotherhood, apparently, gets awkward and embarrassed if anyone mentions its 'Secret Organisation' from the 30s and 40s.

It also means that the Brotherhood is not interested in social radicalism — that is, struggles against inequality, and so on. Very recently, in particular since 2008, when it realised it had missed out on the biggest struggles against Mubarak, it made a turn towards involvement in mass movements. But in any case the Brotherhood is constrained in this regard. In Mahalla, where the big struggles, culminating in 2008, took place, one of the places where workers went on strike is owned by a member of the Ikhwan.

Despite a turn towards social activism, the Brotherhood has no programme for social inequality. Its programme, such as it is, about the economy is flatly bourgeois. Its policy towards the poor is that the rich should be nice to them. (Giving alms to the poor is one of the central duties of Islam: zakat.)

Otherwise, "moderation" meant a turn towards involvement in mainstream, i.e. legal, politics. The Brotherhood has not, until now, been legalised. But it competed in several National Assembly elections — in alliance with the Wafd (the pre-1952 bourgeois nationalist party, which still has a presence of sorts); then the so-called Socialist Labour Party; then, in 2005, as "independents". This election, in which candidates that everyone knew were Brothers, who weren't standing under some other party's umbrella, got 88 seats, represents the high point of this "political" turn.

Apparently there is a conservative wing, currently in the ascendant, which is opposed to this political turn, and thinks "da'wa"— clinics, literacy provision, teaching people to read the Qur'an, etc — is more important. And there is a layer of younger militants who have been influenced by the secular left.

Aside from the big workers' struggles since 2004, and the broad democracy movement represented by the "Kefaya" group (which included Brotherhood representatives), the most visible protests in the last few years have been against the 2003 Gulf War — in which Mubarak supported Bush — and the Israeli wars in Lebanon and Gaza. Mubarak was seen as especially complicit in the Gaza war, because he was seen shaking hands with the Israeli Prime Minister just before Israel's attack began. Some of these mobilisations were very big (50,000 or so), and the Brotherhood was central to them.

Some on the left in Egypt have argued that there is a layer of Ikhwan activists who have been drawn to it, basically, because of the political issues, and not because of Islamist ideology; and that the left, therefore, can relate to them.

It's hard to know. Certainly, it seems to me that an attempt to engage, work with, etc., the base of the Brotherhood — with the intention of breaking them from the movement — is not ruled out. Of course, it would have to be in order to break them, which would require addressing Islamist ideology.

"Neither plague nor cholera!": an open letter to the Socialist Workers' Party

At the start of June 2012 Egyptian activists rallied to remember Khaled Said, a young man killed two years ago by Mubarak's police, sparking protests that eventually brought down the dictator.

At Said's grave, Laila Marzouk, his mother, said she could not bring herself to vote for either of the remaining candidates in Egypt's presidential election: "I will not choose between the plague and cholera."

Those candidates are Ahmed Shafiq, a former prime minister and long-time ally of ousted former president Hosni Mubarak and Mohammed Mursi of the Muslim Brotherhood.

Many of the young activists, trade unionists, leftists and feminists who made the uprising against Mubarak are also dismayed at the choice.

Yet *Socialist Worker* comments: "The choice is clear. A vote for Shafiq would be a vote against the revolution. A vote for Mursi is a vote against the legacy of Mubarak and for continuing change. Now it is time to put Mursi to the test—and to continue struggles over jobs, wages, union rights and for radical political change." (2 June 2012)

But a vote for the right-wing religious sectarians, and fighting for "radical political change," are in flat contradiction.

The SWP-linked Revolutionary Socialists of Egypt appeal to, "all the reformist and revolutionary forces ... to form a national front which stands against the candidate of counter-revolution", and demands that the Muslim Brotherhood declares its commitment to the following:

"1. Formation of a presidential coalition which includes [Nasserite] Hamdeen Sabbahi and ['liberal', salafist-backed Islamist] Abul-Fotouh as Vice-Presidents. 2. The selection of a Prime Minister from outside the ranks of the Brotherhood ... and the formation of a government across the whole political spectrum in which the Copts are represented. 3. The approval of a law on trade union freedoms ... in contrast to the draft law proposed by the Brotherhood to the People's Assembly. 4. The Brotherhood's agreement with other political forces on a civil constitution which guarantees social justice, [etc]"

Workers' Liberty does not advocate voting for Ahmed Shafiq. He is a representative of the old regime and shares political responsibility for the crimes of the Mubarak era.

But no socialist should advocate a vote for the MB, either. The Brotherhood is a right-wing, anti-working-class, religious party. Voting for it contradicts our basic policy of fighting for the independent working-class politics. Worse: the Revolutionary Socialists' four point programme attempts to line-up all left and liberal Egyptian society behind a fantasy programme to press the MB to become an entirely different organisation, or at least to display some pretences and gestures, and link the left into an "agreement" with it.

Since the Brotherhood is the strongest party in Egypt, with a big base in the bourgeoisie as well as in poorer classes, and the left is relatively weak, the "agreement" could only be on the Brotherhood's terms.

SW's positive case for backing the MB in the election seems to rest on the fact that the Islamists oppose the old order, and have a mass base.

The MB is against the old order, but in the name of something at least as bad! If you don't believe what the MB might do, just look at Gaza where their sister party, Hamas, is in power. Hamas has smashed the journalists' union, broken teachers and health workers' strikes, broken up opposition protests with guns, stamped on all organised dissent — including competing Islamists — and imposed conservative social legislation, for example imposing a new 'modest' dress code for schoolgirls.

Hamas has not brought democracy — it has brought its own, authoritarian one-party, clerical rule. It has made a revolution — but its revolution, which is a revolution also against the labour movement, democracy and women's freedom.

And the idea that voting for the MB will represent the continuation of the Egyptian uprising against Mubarak is a re-writing of history.

The MB played a marginal role in the revolution that overthrew Mubarak. At first it refused to participate in the mass demonstrations, only joining — eventually — for fear of losing support.

The MB is not a new, fluid formation created by the uprising against Mubarak. Far from it. It has a long history, going back to 1928. In 1946 Tony Cliff, who would later found the SWP, called it "clerical-fascist": that is how most left-wingers thought of it.

In the 1960s, with the contribution to its ideology of Sayyid Qutb, it became more, not less, insistent on imposing the rules and institutions of an imaginary ideal Islamic past on workers, women, lesbians and gays, freethinkers, and religious minorities.

Illegal or semi-legal for many years in Egypt, and well-rooted now in the wealthy classes, it has learned canniness and tactical flexibility. It knows when and how to display itself as "moderate".

In the last year the MB has attempted to avoid confrontation with the military, which is still hanging on to power. In February, for example, the MB rejected calls for a national strike to bring down the ruling military council. Its counter-campaign was "A day for cleaning Egypt", when it sent its people to clean up litter instead of striking. MB Secretary-General Mahmoud Hussein condemned calls for a general strike, urging the population to double their work rate in order to "rebuild the country and not bring it down."

If Mursi wins, his intention is to immediately strike deals with the IMF and World Bank — as always, such deals will be against the workers.

In the presidential first round Mursi ran a right-wing, religious campaign, aiming for the votes of the salafist (ultra-conservative Islamist) movement. He called himself the only true Islamist in the race, led chants for the implementation of Islamic law, portrayed his political program as a distillation of Islam, occasionally interrupting proceedings with pauses for mass prayer.

Now the MB are shifting their presentation. Murad Mohammed Ali, speaking for the Mursi campaign, states: "We no longer present Mursi as the candidate of the Islamic current but as the candidate of the revolution." The MB has not changed its political nature. It has chosen to change its "image", and dissimulate. But the Revolutionary Socialists take this dissimulation as good coin, and boost it by "demanding" that the Brotherhood continue it.

The Marxist tradition in such conditions is pretty clear: we don't vote for parties such as the MB. Would SW like to revise our past and vote for Peron? or Bhutto's PPP? or the New Deal Democrats? or the Liberals in Britain when they still had the mass workers' vote?

Our job is not to prettify the MB, hold our noses and hope for the best. Our job is to organise those who want to fight. By advocating a vote for the Brothers the SWP / RS discredit themselves among the — numerous — opponents of both the old order and the MB already mobilised in Egypt.

In the late 30s Trotsky made this appeal against lesser-evilism and for independent working class politics: "The whole of [Marx and Lenin's] revolutionary thought was directed towards this: that the fetishism of two camps would give way to a third, independent, sovereign camp of the proletariat, that camp upon which, in point of fact, the future of humanity depends."

Neither Mubarak's henchman, nor the Muslim Brothers, but independent working class politics!

Reassessing imperialism: the case of the 1982 Falklands war

The Falkland Islands, small specks in the South Atlantic, were annexed by Britain and settled by British people in the 1830s. There had been no previous indigenous population.

A century and a half later, in the 1970s and 80s, the islands were an odd little relic of empire. They had no huge economic or strategic importance. Their 1,800 or so inhabitants, many of whom would move on to more clement climates after their time in the Falklands, had no desire to separate from Britain.

Argentina had long laid claim to the islands — calling them the Malvinas — on the grounds that it was the nearest landmass. It was not very near — 400 miles to the islands from the closest point on Argentina's coast, 2,000 miles from Argentina's main population centres. The British population on the islands was longer-settled than the core of the Argentine nation, also European settlers, mostly from Spain and Italy.

The British government found the islands more a nuisance than an asset, and talked with the Argentine government about schemes to link them with Argentina while keeping some special rights.

In early 1982, however, Argentina's military dictators faced mounting popular revolt. They wanted a diversion to regain the initiative. They sent troops to seize the islands on 1-2 April. They hoped that Britain, which had long since abandoned any attempt to be a world military power, would lack motivation and resources to resist.

The British government of Margaret Thatcher did, however, counter-attack; re-took the islands after a short war (25 April to 14 June); and made itself a nice little political coup from the affair. Argentina's military dictator Leopoldo Galtieri resigned three days after the end of the war. His military successor, Reynaldo Bignone, organised elections which brought back civilian government from October 1983. The civilian government brought Galtieri to court for his crimes.

Socialist Organiser, forerunner of *Solidarity*, opposed Britain's war, but denounced the Argentine military's side of the war too. The Falkland islanders had the right to self-determination.

Oddly, in view of its stances today, the Socialist Workers' Party (SWP) had much the same line as the AWL. Later, other leftists also came to scorn

Galtieri's anti-imperialist pretensions — see films such as *Iluminados Por El Fuego* and *Los Chicos De La Guerra*, and the book *Argentina: the Malvinas and the End of Military Rule* by the Argentine Marxists Alejandro Dabat and Luis Lorenzano.

Most would-be revolutionary socialists, however, thought differently. They saw the conflict as one between "imperialism" (Britain) and "anti-imperialism" or at any rate "non-imperialism" (Argentina), and felt duty-bound to take the "anti-imperialist" side.

Inside our organisation at the time, the "back Argentina" view was put by a section led by Alan Thornett, who now supports Socialist Resistance.

Below are extracts from a resolution which summarised the views of our wing of the organisation. The "tendency" referred to in it was a sub-section of the Thornett wing which provided that wing with its theoretical justifications.

The framework of our position was still the "Leninist defeatism" whose historical provenance is an artefact of the Stalinisers of the mid-1920s Communist International, and whose malign work Hal Draper analysed (see *Workers' Liberty* 2/1).The merit of the resolution, which marked a crossroads in the development of the Workers' Liberty tendency, is that it tried to be concrete in its analysis and did not "read off" conclusions from the "epochal position".

Freakish in its origins, at the time the Falklands war appeared to be an episode unlikely to have sequels. Hindsight tells a different story. It posed issues which would be posed again in a number of other wars.

Over Kuwait (1991), Kosova (1999), Afghanistan (2001) and Iraq (2003), wars would be waged by the Western big powers — the "main enemies at home", to use Karl Liebknecht's phrase from World War One, for European and North American socialists — but also ostensibly, and in part really, for aims we supported.

As we supported the Falkland Islanders' freedom, but opposed the British state fighting for that in its own way and with its own concerns in mind, so also we would welcome the expulsion of conquerors from Kuwait, the preservation of the Kosovars' national existence, the ejection of the Taliban, and the ousting of Saddam Hussein, but remain politically hostile to the US-led forces fighting those wars.

The 1982 debate thus has an importance beyond its immediate circumstances.

Britain's war over the Falklands/Malvinas was designed only to preserve a relic of empire and shore up the prestige of British imperialism. A defeatist stand towards Britain's war was therefore the no. 1 campaigning priority for Marxists in Britain.

Instead of assisting the Tories in their crisis by "patriotic" support for the government, the British labour movement should have used the crisis to hasten Thatcher's overthrow in the interests of the working class, and given all material and political support to the Argentine workers in the struggle for democratic and trade union rights and for the establishment of a genuine anti-imperialist workers' government in Argentina.

We repudiate any legitimacy of British territorial claims in the Falklands or any legitimacy in related British claims to resources in Antarctica.

But the pretext on which the Argentine junta embarked upon the invasion of the Falklands/Malvinas was equally contrived. In taking its action, the junta acted not against imperialism, but in a populist ploy designed to divert and unite the Argentine masses behind the Generals' own repressive rule.

In doing so the Argentine dictators trampled upon the rights of the Falkland inhabitants, who in themselves oppress and threaten no-one and should have the right to decide their own future.

Such action did nothing to build anti-imperialist consciousness in the Argentine working class, but rather sought to generate chauvinism and "national unity". We did not support this action, and called for the withdrawal of Argentine troops.

In its seizure of the Falklands/Malvinas, designed to boost its position at home and in the region, the Argentine regime miscalculated about the British reaction, and the US response to the British reaction.

This miscalculation could not however make the seizure, or the war to maintain the seizure, progressive.

Galtieri's invasion did not liberate anyone from colonialism or imperialism. It did not lessen the burden of imperialist exploitation, or improve the conditions for the fight against it, for a single Argentine worker.

It embroiled the Argentine people in a war in which they could hope to win nothing of significance, a disastrous war in a false and reactionary cause.

On both sides therefore the war was reactionary. The job of Marxists in both Britain and Argentina was to oppose the war, to counterpose international working-class unity, to continue the class struggle for the overthrow of both the Tories and the military regime.

Support for the right of the Falkland Islanders — a distinct historical, ethnic, linguistic, economic and geographic community 400 miles from Argentina — to determine their own future is axiomatic for Leninists in the given conditions, where that community exploited no other community, threatened no other community, and was not used as, or likely to be used as, a base for imperialist control of another community.

The Falklanders' right to self-determination cannot be invalidated by their desire to adhere to the now-imperialist state that spawned the Falklands community. That desire to adhere to Britain would invalidate their right to self-determination only if adherence had direct imperialist/colonialist consequences for Argentina or some other country, whose right to resist those consequences would (because of their size, etc.) outweigh the rights of the islanders.

Argentina is far more developed than most non-imperialist countries; it is a fully bourgeois state; and it possesses political independence. It also occupies a subordinate rank within the imperialist world economy. This subordination, however, in no way gives any progressive character to the Argentine bourgeoisie.

The Argentine bourgeoisie is not a progressive force, but the major agency for imperialist domination of the Argentine working class and an assistant for imperialist domination throughout Latin America. It has moreover its own predatory ambitions. For the Argentine working class it is "the main enemy at home". Quite apart from its foreign connections, it is the class that directly exploits them.

We reject as un-Marxist assessments of Argentina's situation such as this:

"Argentina is economically, militarily and politically dominated by imperialism — not by its own national bourgeoisie — but in particular by US interests. The whole basis of its economy is subject to the international market over which Argentina has no influence, let alone control and dominance" (second tendency document, page 2).

We reject the counterposition of the Argentine bourgeoisie to imperialism, and the measuring of Argentina's situation by comparison with a situation where the country would escape the international market (which in a capitalist world it can never do).

Every country is more or less dominated by the world economy. No country has control over it — now not even the US colossus which was supreme after World War Two. This situation cannot be changed by war between the weaker bourgeoisies and the stronger. Not such wars, but the international workers' revolution, can change it.

The communist answer to colonial, semi-colonial and military domination is national liberation struggle; to the domination of the weaker by the strong in the world market (as to the domination of the weak by the strong, and the pauperisation of particular regions, within capitalist nations) our answer is the proletarian revolution.

We emphatically reject the notion that the socialist working class can orientate in world politics, and particularly in relation to conflicts among politically independent capitalist states like Britain and Argentina, by constructing a view of the world in terms of two camps.

"We have to determine our position according to the basic class camps, not on conjunctural events... the class camp into which Argentina fits in a war against imperialism..." (second tendency document, p.4).

The bourgeois foreign policy of the rulers of Argentina, even when it is expressed in acts of war, can in no sense change their class camp.

We reject the notion that military dictatorships in the Third World are simply the creatures of imperialism: that they are strengthened when imperialism is strengthened, weakened when imperialism is weakened.

Military dictatorships are as common in Third World countries which are relatively alienated from the big capitalist powers — Libya, Algeria, Ghana, Ethiopia, Syria, etc. — as in those closely linked to the big capitalist powers (Chile, El Salvador, Nigeria, etc.).

The political regime is fundamentally a product of internal class relations. Frequently, of course, imperialist powers do intervene to prop up or install dictatorships when that suits their purpose. But dictatorial regimes in the Third World are quite capable of pursuing policies hostile to the big capitalist powers without thereby becoming progressive or unleashing a progressive "process". Iran is a clear example.

Argentine workers had no interest in the armed occupation of the Falklands against the wishes of the population; they should have pursued the class struggle regardless of the effects of such struggle on their rulers' ability to maintain the occupation; and it was none of their concern to protect the Argentine bourgeois state against the humiliation it would suffer from being unable to maintain the occupation. These points should have been the basis of Marxist policy in Argentina.

The tactical ways of expressing this principled position could of course be very flexible (following the method according to which Trotskyists developed the "proletarian military policy" as a tactical expression of the defeatist policy in World War Two).

It would be the job of Marxists in Argentina to seek to develop the genuine anti-imperialist elements in the confused nationalist reaction of Argentine workers, with demands such as arming of the workers, expropriation of imperialist property and seizure of the factories.

While making their own views on the war clear, they should have sought to develop common class actions with workers who confusedly saw Argentina's war as "anti-imperialist" but wanted to go further in anti-imperialism.

• From *Solidarity* 241, 11 April 2012

Building a workers' "third front" in Iran

Maziar Razi, **a leading member of the Iranian Revolutionary Marxist Tendency, visited Britain recently and spoke at an informal question-and-answer session organised by Workers' Liberty on 31 May. Notes from Maziar's presentation, taken by** *Daniel Rawnsley*:

Iran has a unique theocratic regime. Other states in the region have called themselves Islamic states, but in Iran, uniquely, the clergy is in power.

How did it come to power? The industrialisation and urbanisation drive by the Shah's regime, linked to the so-called White Revolution, fell into crisis. The clergy wanted concessions from the Shah and were pushed into opposition. They managed to rally millions of petty bourgeois and pauperised petty bourgeois ruined by the economic crisis.

The left in Iran was drawn into the "anti-imperialist", "anti-US" trap of backing Khomeiny. Only two left groups clearly opposed the clergy, Peykar and the forerunner of the IRMT. And we were defeated. The rest of the would-be Marxist left backed Khomeiny. Some even collaborated with him. Some of our comrades became political prisoners within a month of Khomeiny taking power.

The masses who had come on the anti-Shah protests did not want a regime like Khomeiny's to replace the Shah. In 1978-79 we saw the formation of shoras (workers' councils). They organised the general strike which broke the back of the Shah's regime. However, because there was no adequate alternative leadership, even the working class accepted the leadership of the clergy.

The Islamic government has had an internal contradiction from the start. Its medieval ideas are incompatible with modern capitalism. Thus within the regime two tendencies have constantly emerged and re-emerged: the fundamentalists, and more directly pro-capitalist factions which want a quicker deal with the West. Every time the clergy and the fundamentalists eventually reassert control.

Rafsanjani started out in the fundamentalist camp, moved towards pragmatism in power, and was then pushed aside. Within Ahmadinejad's camp now there is a trend seeking a more "moderate" approach to the West.

The issue of Iran's nuclear programme is a secondary one compared to the longstanding internal contradiction. Fundamentally, the clergy have expansionist and sub-imperialist plans in the region.

Despite severe repression, the working class has staged strikes and protests continuously since 1978/79, with the exception only of the early period of the Iran-Iraq war.

"Underground workers' committees" have developed, not tied to individual factories and workplaces. They are based on networks of people who may know each other as friends, family etc. They have been strong enough to organise May Day protests, and resourceful at finding ways to meet and discuss outside the control of the regime.

Politically, however, the activists in the workers' committees have tended to have a syndicalist bent. They'd seen the "Marxists" backing Khomeiny, or turning to terrorist resistance, and they reacted against that.

Our main political challenge has been dealing with that syndicalist bent. We have had to be gradual about introducing the idea of Leninism. We also researched the concept of a "Leninist organisation", and had to rethink it in some ways.

The workers' committee activists have tended to conclude that they cannot bring down the regime, so they should aim to pressurise the regime to get some space in which they can gain concessions on trade-union issues. And in fact the regime has created a tripartite system of industrial negotiation system where a workers' representative meets with a representative of the regime and a representative of the bosses.

The regime doesn't want to give concessions. The syndicalists have fought bravely, but the regime's tactic now is not to kill the worker militants but to exhaust them by repeated prison terms, harassment of their families, etc. It often works. For now the syndicalists are not very active.

We oppose ultra-leftist disdain for the syndicalists. We draw the lesson that organisation has to be clandestine, and that revolutionary organisations must keep their leaders underground.

We also have to go further than the ideas of syndicalism, and demand political freedoms.

How will workers respond if there is war between Iran and Israel or the USA?

At some times during the war with Iraq in the 1980s the regime was very popular. It was difficult for us to advocate our position of refusing to support Iran in the war. We said to workers that they should demand their leaders arm them, rather than volunteer to go and fight under the banner of the regime.

Today the regime is more isolated. Its solid base is around 12% to 15% of the population. These are supporters recruited from poor villages — Basijis — who are given a job that pays well, a house in the city etc. The regime has bought a section of society. They will be with the regime come what may.

But many who have been brutalised by the regime, or had family members raped or killed, are more inclined to welcome the prospect of a US invasion. We say oppose the regime, but don't trust US imperialism, or the Israeli armed forces, to get rid of it. We believe we can construct a third front opposed both to the Iranian regime and to Israel and the US.

There is a good chance that a nationalist tendency will exist when imperialists attack, but the reactionary nature of the regime will limit it. A few years ago people demonstrated in great numbers in support of the reformists, and the regime responded with extreme brutality. A very deep hatred towards the regime exists in the population.

However, at present I think war is unlikely.

You can compare Iran with 1930s fascist states in Europe in some way, but there is a big difference between Iran and even the "clerical-fascist" regimes of the 1930s like Spain and Portugal: the clergy holds state power. In modern history elsewhere we haven't seen the clergy come to power; it has been on the sidelines supporting the regime.

The percentage of business that is state owned is still very high, around 70%, despite a privatisation policy, and although it is difficult to get precise figures.

Economic sanctions have had an effect. Some factories have stopped producing because they can no longer get supplies. The most important industries are state owned: oil, petrochemicals). The biggest struggles take place in the car industry. Iran Khodro employs around 30,000 workers, and workers have won disputes there.

Turkish comrades whom we have discussed with [Marksist Tutum] argue that "sub-imperialism" has emerged, and cite Iran and Turkey as examples. Certainly Iran has a different position in the world from, say, Bangladesh. We need to discuss the Turkish comrades' ideas more, but they seem to make sense.

The majority of people are religious and observant. Many syndicalists whom we have worked with are religious, and argue that the regime is not truly Islamic. Religion is stronger in the villages. Young people in Tehran, especially women, tend not to be devout. Young women bend the strict dress codes.

The situation is also different in Kurdistan. There, people have a history of resistance to the regime, and the political situation is more open.

The regime restricts the internet, reducing connection speeds at certain times for example, and monitoring people's usage. But Facebook has helped us a great deal. We were able to use the internet to start discussions and meet some social democrats and anarchists online. We formed a Marxist sub-group to start discussions on the *Communist Manifesto*, and people in this online group set up physical groups where they live.

Twitter and Facebook have been important for demonstrations. During the protests two years ago the regime cut off mobile phone use.

• From *Solidarity* 248, 6 June 2012

INTRODUCTION TO MARXISM
What is capitalism?

By Karl Marx

Capital consists of raw materials, instruments of labour, and means of subsistence of all kinds, which are employed in producing new raw materials, new instruments, and new means of subsistence. All these components of capital are created by labour, products of labour, accumulated labour. Accumulated labour that serves as a means to new production is capital.

So say the economists.

What is a Negro slave? A man of the black race. The one explanation is worthy of the other.

A Negro is a Negro. Only under certain conditions does he become a slave. A cotton-spinning machine is a machine for spinning cotton. Only under certain conditions does it become capital. Torn away from these conditions, it is as little capital as gold is itself money, or sugar is the price of sugar.

In the process of production, human beings work not only upon nature, but also upon one another. They produce only by working together in a specified manner and reciprocally exchanging their activities. In order to produce, they enter into definite connections and relations to one another, and only within these social connections and relations does their influence upon nature operate — i.e., does production take place.

These social relations between the producers, and the conditions under which they exchange their activities and share in the total act of production, will naturally vary according to the character of the means of production. With the discover of a new instrument of warfare, the firearm, the whole internal organization of the army was necessarily altered, the relations within which individuals compose an army and can work as an army were transformed, and the relation of different armies to another was likewise changed.

We thus see that the social relations within which individuals produce, the social relations of production, are altered, transformed, with the change and development of the material means of production, of the forces of production. The relations of production in their totality constitute what is called the social relations, society, and, moreover, a society at a definite stage of historical development, a society with peculiar, distinctive characteristics. Ancient society, feudal society, bourgeois (or capitalist) society, are such totalities of relations of production, each of which denotes a particular stage of development in the history of mankind.

Capital also is a social relation of production. It is a bourgeois relation of production, a relation of production of bourgeois society. The means of subsistence, the instruments of labour, the raw materials, of which capital consists — have they not been produced and accumulated under given social conditions, within definite special relations? Are they not employed for new production, under given special conditions, within definite social relations? And does not just the definite social character stamp the products which serve for new production as capital?

Capital consists not only of means of subsistence, instruments of labour, and raw materials, not only as material products; it consists just as much of exchange values. All products of which it consists are commodities. Capital, consequently, is not only a sum of material products, it is a sum of commodities, of exchange values, of social magnitudes.

Capital remains the same whether we put cotton in the place of wool, rice in the place of wheat, steamships in the place of railroads, provided only that the cotton, the rice, the steamships — the body of capital — have the same exchange value, the same price, as the wool, the wheat, the railroads, in which it was previously embodied. The bodily form of capital may transform itself continually, while capital does not suffer the least alteration...

The existence of a class which possesses nothing but the ability to work is a necessary presupposition of capital.

It is only the dominion of past, accumulated, materialised labour over immediate living labour that stamps the accumulated labour with the character of capital.

Capital does not consist in the fact that accumulated labour serves living labour as a means for new production. It consists in the fact that living labour serves accumulated labour as the means of preserving and multiplying its exchange value...Does a worker in a cotton factory produce only cotton? No. He produces capital. He produces values which serve anew to command his work and to create by means of it new values.

Capital can multiply itself only by exchanging itself for labour-power, by calling wage-labour into life. The labour-power of the wage-labourer can exchange itself for capital only by increasing capital, by strengthening that very power whose slave it is. Increase of capital, therefore, is increase of the proletariat, i.e., of the working class.

And so, the bourgeoisie and its economists maintain that the interest of the capitalist and of the labourer is the same. And in fact, so they are! The worker perishes if capital does not keep him busy. Capital perishes if it does not exploit labour-power, which, in order to exploit, it must buy. The more quickly the capital destined for production — the productive capital — increases, the more prosperous industry is, the more the bourgeoisie enriches itself, the better business gets, so many more workers does the capitalist need, so much the dearer does the worker sell himself. The fastest possible growth of productive capital is, therefore, the indispensable condition for a tolerable life to the labourer.

But what is growth of productive capital? Growth of the power of accumulated labour over living labour; growth of the rule of the bourgeoisie over the working class. When wage-labour produces the alien wealth dominating it, the power hostile to it, capital, there flow back to it its means of employment – i.e., its means of subsistence, under the condition that it again become a part of capital, that is become again the lever whereby capital is to be forced into an accelerated expansive movement.

To say that the interests of capital and the interests of the workers are identical, signifies only this: that capital and wage-labour are two sides of one and the same relation. The one conditions the other in the same way that the usurer and the borrower condition each other.

As long as the wage-labourer remains a wage-labourer, his lot is dependent upon capital. That is what the boasted community of interests between worker and capitalists amounts to.

If capital grows, the mass of wage-labour grows, the number of wage-workers increases; in a word, the sway of capital extends over a greater mass of individuals.

Let us suppose the most favourable case: if productive capital grows, the demand for labour grows. It therefore increases the price of labour-power, wages.

A house may be large or small; as long as the neighbouring houses are likewise small, it satisfies all social requirement for a residence. But let there arise next to the little house a palace, and the little house shrinks to a hut. The little house now makes it clear that its inmate has no social position at all to maintain, or but a very insignificant one; and however high it may shoot up in the course of civilization, if the neighbouring palace rises in equal or even in greater measure, the occupant of the relatively little house will always find himself more uncomfortable, more dissatisfied, more cramped within his four walls.

An appreciable rise in wages presupposes a rapid growth of productive capital. Rapid growth of productive capital calls forth just as rapid a growth of wealth, of luxury, of social needs and social pleasures. Therefore, although the pleasures of the labourer have increased, the social gratification which they afford has fallen in comparison with the increased pleasures of the capitalist, which are inaccessible to the worker, in comparison with the stage of development of society in general.Our wants and pleasures have their origin in society; we therefore measure them in relation to society; we do not measure them in relation to the objects which serve for their gratification. Since they are of a social nature, they are of a relative nature.

• *From Wage Labour and Capital*

The past, present and future of the trade unions
By Karl Marx

a. Their past.

Capital is concentrated social force, while the workman has only to dispose of his working force. The contract between capital and labour can therefore never be struck on equitable terms, equitable even in the sense of a society which places the ownership of the material means of life and labour on one side and the vital productive energies on the opposite side. The only social power of the workmen is their number. The force of numbers, however is broken by disunion. The disunion of the workmen is created and perpetuated by their unavoidable competition among themselves.

Trades Unions originally sprang up from the spontaneous attempts of workmen at removing or at least checking that competition, in order to conquer such terms of contract as might raise them at least above the condition of mere slaves. The immediate object of Trades Unions was therefore confined to everyday necessities, to expediences for the obstruction of the incessant encroachments of capital, in one word, to questions of wages and time of labour. This activity of the Trades Unions is not only legitimate, it is necessary. It cannot be dispensed with so long as the present system of production lasts. On the contrary, it must be generalised by the formation and the combination of Trades Unions throughout all countries. On the other hand, unconsciously to themselves, the Trades Unions were forming centres of organisation of the working class, as the mediaeval municipalities and communes did for the middle class. If the Trades Unions are required for the guerilla fights between capital and labour, they are still more important as organised agencies for superseding the very system of wages labour and capital rule.

b. Their present

Too exclusively bent upon the local and immediate struggles with capital, the Trades Unions have not yet fully understood their power of acting against the system of wages slavery itself. They therefore kept too much aloof from general social and political movements...

c. Their future.

Apart from their original purposes, they must now learn to act deliberately as organising centres of the working class in the broad interest of its complete emancipation. They must aid every social and political movement tending in that direction. Considering themselves and acting as the champions and representatives of the whole working class, they cannot fail to enlist the non-society men into their ranks. They must look carefully after the interests of the worst paid trades, such as the agricultural labourers, rendered powerless incapable of organised resistance by exceptional circumstances. They must convince the broad masses of workers that their efforts, far from being narrow and selfish, aim at the emancipation of the downtrodden millions.

• From the General Council's report to the Geneva congress of the First International, 1866. By Karl Marx

Why is the left so divided?
By Max Shachtman

To put it briefly, a revolutionary socialist party is needed to win the working class to the principles of socialism, to so-called socialist methods of struggle against capitalist exploitations and oppression, and finally to the socialist victory itself. Socialism will never come by itself. It must be fought for. Without an organised, conscious, disciplined, active revolutionary socialist party, the triumph of socialism is impossible.

The Workers Party [the group Shachtman and others founded when they broke from the American SWP — no relation to the British group — in 1939/40] is not the only political organisation which advocates socialism. There are several parties which proclaim the same goal. This is often very confusing to a worker. He will say: "How am I to tell which party is the right one for me to join or support?" Or, "Why don't all those who are in favour of socialism unite into a single party?" Or, "If you cannot agree among yourselves, how do you expect me to agree with any of you?"

It should not be too hard to answer these questions. When a worker learns that a tool is useful and necessary, he does not throw up his hands in despair merely because there are many varieties of that tool offered to him. He reads carefully the claims made for each party and the description given of what it can do, and he judges from experience which one really serves the purpose best.

If there is sickness in the family, he learns that there are all sorts of "schools" of healing. One insists that illness can be cured by the science of modern medicine; another emphasises adjustment of the bones; still another, pressure on nerve centres; a fourth, treatment by sun rays; a fifth, treatment by the faith of mind and heart; and there are the believers in cures by magic incantations and movements of the hand. He would not, because of all this, cry out: "Why don't they all get together on the question of cures?" Or, "How am I to tell which to choose?" Instead, he would examine to the best of his ability the methods and the results of each "school," making the most scientific possible test of which is most scientific.

It is not so very much different in politics. To judge the different parties, it is necessary to check on their words and their deeds. That is, to examine the programmes of the different parties, what they are for and what they are against, and to see if what they do in practice corresponds to what they say in words. On that basis, it is easy to conclude which one best serves the interests of socialism.

• From *The Fight for Socialism*, 1946

What is socialism?
By Frederick Engels

Their political and intellectual bankruptcy is scarcely any longer a secret to the bourgeoisie themselves. Their economic bankruptcy recurs regularly every 10 years. In every crisis, society is suffocated beneath the weight of its own productive forces and products, which it cannot use, and stands helpless, face-to-face with the absurd contradiction that the producers have nothing to consume, because consumers are wanting.

The expansive force of the means of production burst the bonds that the capitalist mode of production had imposed upon them. Their deliverance from these bonds is the one precondition for an unbroken, constantly-accelerated development of the productive forces, and therewith for a practically unlimited increase of production itself.

Nor is this all. The socialised appropriation of the means of production does away, not only with the present artificial restrictions upon production, but also with the positive waste and devastation of productive forces and products that are at the present time the inevitable concomitants of production, and that reach their height in the crises. Further, it sets free for the community at large a mass of means of production and of products, by doing away with the senseless extravagance of the ruling classes of today, and their political representatives.

The possibility of securing for every member of society, by means of socialised production, an existence not only fully sufficient materially, and becoming day-by-day more full, but an existence guaranteeing to all the free development and exercise of their physical and mental faculties — this possibility is now, for the first time, here, but it is here.

With the seizing of the means of production by society, production of commodities is done away with, and, simultaneously, the mastery of the product over the producer. Anarchy in social production is replaced by systematic, definite organization. The struggle for individual existence disappears.

Then, for the first time, humanity, in a certain sense, is finally marked off from the rest of the animal kingdom, and emerges from mere animal conditions of existence into really human ones. The whole sphere of the conditions of life which environ humanity, and which have hitherto ruled humanity, now comes under the dominion and control of humanity, who for the first time becomes the real, conscious lord of nature, because it has now become master of its own social organization.

The laws of its own social action, hitherto standing face-to-face with humanity as laws of Nature foreign to, and dominating it, will then be used with full understanding, and so mastered by it. humanity's own social organisation, hitherto confronting it as a necessity imposed by Nature and history, now becomes the result of its own free action. The extraneous objective forces that have, hitherto, governed history, pass under the control of humanity itself.

Only from that time will humanity itself, more and more consciously, make its own history — only from that time will the social causes set in movement by it have, in the main and in a constantly growing measure, the results intended by it. It is the ascent of humanity from the kingdom of necessity to the kingdom of freedom.

• From *Socialism Utopian and Scientific*